John James Kehoe

The municipal councillors' hand-book

John James Kehoe

The municipal councillors' hand-book

ISBN/EAN: 9783742876270

Manufactured in Europe, USA, Canada, Australia, Japa

Cover: Foto ©Thomas Meinert / pixelio.de

Manufactured and distributed by brebook publishing software (www.brebook.com)

John James Kehoe

The municipal councillors' hand-book

THE
MUNICIPAL COUNCILLORS'
HAND-BOOK.

BEING A SUMMARY OF THE

Municipal Law of Ontario,

FOR GENERAL PUBLIC USE.

BY J. JAMES KEHOE,

OF OSGOODE HALL, BARRISTER-AT-LAW,

Author of "A Treatise on the Law of Choses in Action."

1884.
PRATT & TRACY, PUBLISHERS,
STRATFORD, ONT.

PREFACE.

At different times the author had received suggestions from Councillors and others, urging upon him the publication of such a work as the present. Acting upon these suggestions he has undertaken the task and the result of his labors is now before the public.

This book will be found to contain the various points of municipal law on which people generally wish to be informed. In such a small compass, the subject cannot be treated in anything like an exhaustive manner, for the reader must consider that in the great work known as Harrison's Municipal Manual the lamented and distinguished author complains that his closely printed work of over 1100 pages is incomplete. Harrison's Manual, besides being too extensive for the general reader, is also a work which hardly any one else than a lawyer can in great part well understand. This work is devoted to those who wish to be informed on the most general parts of municipal law. For this purpose it is written in plain language, free from legal technicalities.

The present work is brief and condensed. Any one who has ever tried the work of condensation will agree that it is a very difficult kind of work, far more difficult than elaboration. Being condensed, there will be found in the following pages a large amount of matter. The author has endeavored to bring in everything that could be of interest, at the same time confining it to the small compass into which it is compressed. From the consolidated Municipal Act of 1883, and other statutes, as well as from the decisions of the Courts, the subject matter has been taken. The plan of the chapters, it will be observed by those who consult the Act of 1883, follows the plan of that Act as closely as possible. This has been done for the convenience of those who wish to refer to the Act in connection with this work. References to authorities and legal decisions, and where they are cited from, have been designedly omitted, as the persons for whom the work is intended are not possessed of law libraries. Those who do consult the Act in connection with this book, will find that matter which would fill several pages has here been stated in a few lines, with nothing material omitted. Where the particular wording of a statute was found to be of importance, it has been closely followed.

During the progress of the work the author has been asked if it would contain the law relating to schools, the assessment law, etc.; it does not contain all these subjects. To do this would be far beyond its scope, and would require (if the various expectations of people were realized) a work of a dozen volumes much larger than this. The present work is simply what its title implies,—a Municipal Councillors' Hand-book.

It is the hope of the author that it will fill a sphere of usefulness of its own. This is, to make those who read it, familiar at least in a general way, with the various components of our municipal system. We enjoy in this province a system which has been pronounced by the late Chief Justice Harrison, to be the greatest known to him. One element of it, as it appears to the author is, that very large powers being given to municipalities and Councillors being familiarized with public affairs, in a very full manner, a large section of the people have their share in important public concerns. These public concerns are brought home closely to the people, and the effect of this is to make us all appreciate the free institutions with which we are blessed in this young country above all other countries, and to beget amongst us a public spirit.

The general municipal law is here given, not that relating to particular municipalities, which have special Acts relating to themselves. Again, as villages known as Police Villages are so very few (there being, as far as can be learned, only a half dozen in the province) nothing is said about them.

The author is indebted to Mr. John Idington, Q. C., for having revised the proof sheets of the book, and for having received from him several valuable suggestions from time to time. These have made the book more valuable than it would otherwise be.

J. JAMES KEHOE.

STRATFORD, *January, 1884.*

TABLE OF CONTENTS.

	PAGE
DEDICATION	3
PREFACE	5
CALENDAR	12
ERRATA	16

CHAPTER I.

CONSTITUTION OF MUNICIPALITIES	17
Formation of Villages	18
" Towns and Cities	20
Separation of Town from County	22
Re-union of Town and County	23
Townships	23
Counties	25
General Matters Consequent on the Formation of New Corporations	26

CHAPTER II.

THE MEMBERS OF MUNICIPAL COUNCILS—THEIR QUALIFICATIONS, DISQUALIFICATION AND EXEMPTIONS	30
Composition of Municipal Councils	30
Qualifications	33
Disqualification	34
Exemptions	37

CHAPTER III.

MUNICIPAL ELECTIONS	38
Nominations	38
Rules as to Time and Place of Election	40
Who are Qualified to Vote?	43
The Returning Officers and Deputy-Returning Officers	46
Oaths	47
The Polling	52

CHAPTER IV.

MEETINGS OF COUNCILS—VACANCIES IN COUNCILS	63
Duties of Officers	63
Declarations of Qualification	64

Conduct of Business	66
Rules of Order	68
Vacancies in Council	71

CHAPTER V.

MUNICIPAL OFFICERS	74
The Head of the Council	74
The Clerk	74
The Treasurer	78
Assessors and Collectors	80
Auditors	81
Powers to Administer Oaths	82
Salaries of Officers	83

CHAPTER VI.

GENERAL POWER OF ALL MUNICIPALITIES	85
By-Laws	87
Confirmation of By-Laws	95
By-Laws Creating Debts	96
Anticipatory Appropriations	103
Finances	105

CHAPTER VII.

ARBITRATIONS	106

CHAPTER VIII.

POLICE OFFICE, MAGISTRATE, COMMISSIONERS, ETC., IN CITIES AND TOWNS—COURT HOUSE, GAOLS, ETC.	110
Police Commissioners	111
Court Houses, Gaols, etc.	112

CHAPTER IX.

INVESTIGATION INTO THE CONDUCT OF OFFICIALS	117

CHAPTER X.

POWERS OF PARTICULAR MUNICIPAL COUNCILS	118
Powers of Councils of Counties, Townships, Cities, Towns and Villages	119
Powers of Councils of Townships and Cities	125
" Councils of Counties and Cities	135
" Councils of Counties, Cities and Separated Towns	136
Powers of Councils of Cities, Towns and Villages	138
" Councils of Cities and Towns	147

Powers of Councils of Townships, Towns and Villages	149
Powers of Councils of Towns and Villages	149
Exclusive Powers of Councils of Townships	152

CHAPTER XI.

HIGHWAYS AND BRIDGES	154
General Provisions	154
Powers of Counties, Townships, Cities, Towns and Villages in relation to Roads and Bridges	162
Powers of Townships, Cities, Towns and Villages	165
" County Councils	167
" Township Councils	16

CHAPTER XII.

DRAINAGE AND OTHER LOCAL IMPROVEMENTS	171
Townships, Cities, Towns and Villages	171
Cities, Towns and Villages	178
County By-Laws for Road Improvements	185

CHAPTER XIII.

POWERS OF MUNICIPAL COUNCILS AS TO RAILWAYS	188
INDEX	191

MUNICIPAL CALENDAR.

NOTE.—Where not otherwise mentioned the references are to the sections of the Municipal Act of 1883. See also Index at end of this book for matters referred to in this Calendar.

JANUARY.

January 1.—Yearly taxes are to be computed from this date, unless otherwise ordered. (Sec. 366.)

10.—Last day for return to be transmitted to Provincial Secretary by Clerk of Municipality issuing Debentures. (Sec. 3 of Rev. Stat. Ont. Chap. 176.)

15.—Last day for Treasurer of a Municipality indebted to Municipal Loan Fund to make returns to Provincial Treasurer. (Sec. 383.)

30.—Owners of unoccupied lands to send their name, residence and address on or before this day, so as to avoid being assessed as non-residents. (Sec. 8 Rev. Stat. Ont., chap. 180.)

31.—Last day for every Council to make yearly report to the Provincial Secretary of corporation debts. (Sec. 88.)

Last day for auditors to discharge their duties. (Sec. 270.)

FOR DAYS OF THE WEEK IN JANUARY.

On first Monday in January, members of Councils to be elected. (Secs. 88 and 89.)

All Municipal Councils (except County Councils) to meet on third Monday in January, at eleven o'clock a.m. (Sec. 221.)

County Councils hold their first meeting on fourth Tuesday in January, at two o'clock p.m. (Sec. 221.)

County Treasurer to submit to the County Council a report, certified by the auditors, of the non-resident land fund, at its first session in January. (Rev. Stat. Ont. Chap. 180, sec. 182.)

High School and Collegiate Institute Trustees to be appointed by Councils at their first meeting, to be held after the first of January in each year. (Rev. Stat. Ont., Chap. 205, sec 20.)

FEBRUARY.

February 1.—On or before this day, Railway Companies are to furnish annually certain statements to Clerks of Municipalities. (See Rev. Stat Ont., Chap. 180, Sec. 26).

On or before this day Clerks are to make up and deliver to Assessors lists of persons requiring their names to be entered on the roll, and the lands owned by them. (Rev. Stat. Ont., Chap. 180, sec. 3.)

On or before this day, County, City and Town Treasurers

to furnish Clerks with lists of lands in arrears for taxes for three years. (Rev. Stat. Ont., Chap. 180, sec. 118.)

15.—Assessors to begin to make up their rolls not later than this day. (Rev. Stat. Ont., Chap 180, sec. 42.)

28th or 29th in leap year.—Last day for Councils to impose larger duty up to $200 for Tavern or Shop Licenses. (Rev. Stat. Ont., Chap., 181, sec. 32.)

Last day for City, Town, Village or Township Councils to limit the number of Shop and Tavern Licenses and to confine Shop Licenses exclusively to the sale of liquor. (Rev. Stat. Ont., Chap. 181, secs. 17 and 24.

Last day for City or Town Councils to prescribe further requirements for Taverns. (Rev. Stat. Ont., Chap. 181, sec. 21.)

In this month the Commissioner of Crown Lands is required to transmit to County Treasurers, a list of all the lands within the County located as free grants, sold or agreed to be sold by the Crown or leased, or in respect of which a license of occupation issued during the preceding year. (Rev. Stat. Ont., Chap. 180, sec. 106.)

In this month petition for separation of Counties must be made. (Sec. 38.)

MARCH.

March 1.—Within one week after this date every Town, Village and Township Clerk must make a return of certain particulars (mentioned on page 76 of work) to the County Treasurer. (Sec. 247.)

31.—Similar return to be made on or before this day by Clerks of Cities and Towns separated from Counties to the Provincial Secretary. (Sec. 249.)

Similar return with additions to be made on or before this day by County Treasurers to the Provincial Secretary. (Sec. 248.)

APRIL.

April 8.—Last day for township and village clerks to furnish county treasurers with the statement of arrears of taxes and school rates on non-resident lands afterwards occupied. (Rev. Stat. Ont. chap. 180, sec. 113)

30.—Last day for Assessor to complete roll. (Rev. Stat.) Ont. chap. 180, sec. 42.)

MAY.

May 1.—Last day for Assessors to deliver their rolls completed and added up to the clerks, certificates and affidavits to be attached. (Rev. Stat. Ont. chap. 180, sec. 43.)

Last day for non-residents to complain of assessment, (Rev. Stat. Ont. chap. 180, sec. 67).

County Treasurers to report to clerks that any land liable to assessment has not been assessed, etc (Rev. Stat. Ont. chap. 180, sec. 121.)

JUNE.

June 30.—License Commissioners and Inspector to pay

over to Treasurer of municipality two-thirds of license fees, after deducting expenses of Inspector, office of License Commissioners and of enforcing law. (Rev. Stat. Ont. chap. 181, sec. 34.)

JUNE.

June 30.—Last day for revision of assessment rolls by Court of Revision. (Rev. Stat. Ont. chap. 180, sec. 56, sub. sec. 19).

Last day for equalization of assessment rolls by County Councils. (Rev. Stat. Ont. chap. 180, sec. 68).

Last day for County Councils to pass by-laws for nominations in townships, to be on last Monday but one in December. (Sec. 112)

JULY.

July 1.—Last day for County Treasurer to return to clerks of local municipalities an account of all arrears of taxes due in respect of non-resident lands which have become occupied. (Rev. Stat. Ont. chap. 180, sec. 111.)

Last day for city or town treasurer to perform the same duty. (Same section.)

Before or after this day Court of Revision may reduce or remit taxes in certain cases. (Rev. Stat. Ont. chap. 180, sec. 58.)

5. Last day for serving notice of appeal from Court of Revision to County Judge. (Rev. Stat. Ont., chap. 180, sec. 59, sub-sec. 2.)

14. Last day for city or town Councils to pass resolutions affirming the expediency of a new division into Wards. (Sec. 21.)

AUGUST.

August 14.—Last day for County Clerks to certify to local clerks amounts required for county purposes. (Rev. Stat. Ont. chap. 180, sec. 74.)

August 14.—Last day for Overseer of Highways to return to clerk of municipality name of non-resident as defaulter who does not perform his statute labour. (Rev. Stat. Ont. chap. 180, sec. 87.)

SEPTEMBER.

September 1.—On or before this day Assessors to return their rolls for jury purposes. (Rev. Stat. Ont. chap. 180, sec. 194.)

OCTOBER.

October 1.—Last day for return of assessment roll to city or town clerk in cities or towns where assessment regulated to take place between 1st July and 30th September. (Rev. Stat. Ont. chap. 180, sec. 44.)

On or before this day clerks to deliver to collectors collectors' rolls, unless some other day be prescribed by a by-law of the local municipality. (Rev. Stat. Ont. chap. 180, sec. 89.

30.—Last day for County Council to pass a by-law for

holding first election in junior county after separation. (Sec. 91.)

NOVEMBER.

November 1.—On or before this day local clerks to transmit to County Treasurer rolls of lands of non-residents whose names are not on assessment rolls. (Rev. Stat. Ont chap. 180, sec. 90.)

9.—Last day for collectors to demand taxes of lands omitted from the roll found due under sec. 121 of Rev. Stat. Ont. chap. 180.

15.—Courts of Revision in cities and towns separated from county to close this day, when assessment regulated to take place between 1st July and 30th September. (Rev. Stat. Ont. chap. 180, sec. 44)

DECEMBER.

December 1.—Last day for Councils to hear and determine appeals, under sec. 121 of Re v. Stat. Ont. chap. 180, of lands omitted from the Assessment Roll.

On or before this day clerks of every city, town, village and township are to transmit a true return of the number of resident ratepayers appearing on the revised Assessment Rolls of their municipalities. (Sec. 246.)

13.—Last day for payment of taxes in cities, towns, villages and townships passing by-laws for the purpose. (Sec. 490, sub-sec. 2.)

14.—On or before this day collectors to return their rolls and pay over proceeds. Councils may appoint a later day up to the 1st of February in the next year. (Rev. Stat. Ont. chap. 180, sec. 101.)

15.—On this day collectors to make returns to Treasurers (when taxes are required to be paid before the 14th December) names of all persons who have not paid taxes. (Sec. 256, sub-sec. 3.)

19.—Last day for Treasurers to prepare and transmit to clerks (in municipalities where a by-law is passed to pay taxes before the 14th December) a list of persons who have not paid taxes. (Sec 254.)

FOR DAYS OF THE WEEK IN DECEMBER.

On last Monday nomination of candidates as follows:—

For Mayors in cities, and for Mayors, Reeves and Deputy-Reeves in towns at 10 o'clock a. m.

For Aldermen in cities, Councillors in towns, and Reeves, Deputy-Reeves and Councillors in townships and villages at noon.

For Reeves in townships divided into Wards at 10 a.m.

For Councillors in townships divided into Wards at noon. (Sees. 107, 109 and 110.)

If the last Monday falls or Christmas day the above nominations take place on the preceding Friday instead. (Sec. 111.)

ERRATA.

The following errors occurred in the printing of the book:

Page 21.—Line 17 should read "The town so reduced should not have less than 2,000 inhabitants."

Page 34.—The following lines were omitted after the 4th line from the bottom of the page.

"But if within any township a person is at the time of election in actual occupation of such freehold rated in his own name on the last revised assessment roll, he will be qualified if the freehold is rated in the roll not less than $4,000, and any lien or encumbrance has no effect."

Page 87.—Line 11 from the top of the page is misprinted in some copies; it should read:—"It would be a safe rule to insist on the seal being applied in open Council."

Page 118.—"Chapter VIII" should read "Chapter X."

Page 171.—The Sub-heading "Division I.—Townships, Cities and Villages" should read to include "Towns."

MUNICIPAL COUNCILLORS' HAND-BOOK.

CHAPTER I.
CONSTITUTION OF MUNICIPALITIES.

In Ontario municipal corporations derive their existence from the Municipal Act ; in England they were created by old charters granted at various times, some of them having a very early history. The peculiar qualities of a corporation, whether a municipal corporation or an incorporated company are that it has a continual existence, which may be prolonged for an indefinite time, and secondly, though the corporation is composed of many persons, it may act as a single individual.

Yet when it is said that a corporation may act as an individual, it must be understood that there are certain formalities required for most of its acts. Thus it is an ordinary rule that every corporation must have a seal, and contracts made by it, must be under such seal. Another method of carrying on its proceedings is by the system of by-law. These formal matters will be treated of in a later chapter of this work. We will now explain the formation of the different kinds of municipal corporations as they exist in this province.

I.—FORMATION OF VILLAGES.

The formation of a village is within the power of County Councils.

The requisites are as follows:—

1. The taking of a census by which it must appear that the intended village contains 750 inhabitants.

2. A petition to the County Council or Councils must be made by at least 100 residents, freeholders and householders of the village, of whom one-half must be freeholders.

3. By-law of the County Council or Councils creating the village, giving it its name, defining its boundaries, and appointing the time for the first election to take place, and also the returning officer.

If the village has less than 1,000 inhabitants, its area must not be more than 500 acres. This area can not be afterwards increased except at the rate of 200 acres for every additional thousand persons. The land occupied by streets and public squares is not to be considered as part of the area when *extending* the limits of the village. The law is not clear as to how squares and streets are to be taken when the village is formed originally, whether they should be included as part of the first 500 acres or not. The better opinion would seem to be that they should not in this case be included.

With regard to the subject of extension of villages just alluded to, this may be done by the Lieutenant-Governor on petition of the village council.

When the newly incorporated village lies within two or more counties, the County Councils should by by-law annex the village to one of the counties. If this be not done within six months, the Wardens are required to notify the Provincial Lieutenant-Governor-in-Council, setting forth the grounds of difference between the County Councils, and thereupon it is the duty of the Lieutenant-Governor-in-Council to annex the village to one of the counties.

In the event of the Wardens neglecting to notify the Lieutenant-Governor-in-Council, then one hundred freeholders and householders on the census list of the village, may, within one month after the six months have expired, memorialize the Lieutenant-Governor. The Lieutenant-Governor may act upon such memorial by annexing the village to either County.

When a portion of an incorporated village is by any of the above methods taken from one county and annexed to another it becomes necessary that the share of the county debt belonging to the part so detached, should be borne by the county to which it is annexed. The municipal act provides machinery for this purpose.

A village may be lessened in area as well as increased. This is done by a by-law of the County Council upon petition of the village council. To effect this, the village must not have any more debt than double its last annual tax rate, and the population must not be reduced below 750 people, nor can municipal rights or privileges of the village be interfered with.

The land so cut off must be only such land as is used for farming purposes.

In 1888 the Legislature passed an act by which a village may cease to be incorporated. This is done, firstly, by a vote of two-thirds of the village council, and such resolution being adopted by a vote of the ratepayers. Then it is necessary that an adjoining municipality or municipalities, as the case may be, should by resolution approve of the annexation of the unincorporated village, and lastly, the Lieutenant-Governor completes the act by a proclamation.

If the territory of the unincorporated village is annexed to two or more municipalities, these must by agreement or arbitration, fix among themselves the proportion of the village debts to be borne by them, as well as the share of the assets acquired from the village.

The part which comprised the village may be charged for a time with a special rate or relieved of any rate, by the municipality or municipalities to which it is annexed.

A *village* or *town* may be annexed to an adjacent *village, town* or *city* by mutual resolutions of the municipalities concerned.

II.—FORMATION OF TOWNS AND CITIES.

A village or town council may at any time pass a by-law to have a census taken. When a village has 2,000 of a population it may become a town, and when a town reaches 15,000,* it may become a city. The method of proceeding is by the village or town council advertising a notice in a newspaper of the village or town for three months. The notice sets forth the intention to become a town or city as the case may be, and describes the limits. The head of the corporation must send a certified census return, and prove the publication of the notice to the Lieu-

---

*It has been usual for towns of 10,000 of population to apply to the Legislature for a special act of incorporation as cities.

tenant-Governor. The latter, by making a proclamation, causes the change to be made.

If the village or town has no newspaper, then the notice is to be inserted in the newspaper in the county town, and four notices are in such case required to be posted up in four of the most public places in the village or town. When a town becomes incorporated, the County Treasurer makes a list of all arrears of taxes in the newly incorporated Town, and transmits it to the treasurer of the Town. The Town Treasurer has then the same power to collect these arrears as the Warden and County Treasurer had before.

The area of a Town not separated from the County may be reduced by the County Council in the same manner as that of a village.

The town so reduced in area must have less than 2,000 inhabitants.

In the case of a Town becoming a City, there must be a settlement of the debts between it and the County. In case of disagreement, the settlement is arrived at by arbitration.

Arbitrations are specially treated of in a subsequent chapter.

There are no Wards in Villages, but every Town or City must have at least three Wards. Each Ward must have at least 500 inhabitants.

The number of Wards may be increased at any time before the 15th July in any year, by a vote of two-thirds of the Council. This two-thirds means of the whole Council, not simply those who may be present at a meeting. It is done by resolution, not by by-law. The difference between a by law and a resolution is that the former must be under the seal of the Corporation, and the latter requires no seal.

III.—SEPARATION OF TOWN FROM COUNTY.

A Town may at any time separate from the County. It must first pass a by-law for the purpose, and this by-law must receive the assent of the electors.

In carrying out such separation, the town must settle with the County for the following matters:

1. Expenses of Administration of Justice.
2. Use of the Gaol.
3. Erection and repair of Registry office.
4. Books for Registry offices, and for services for which County is liable under the Registry Act.
5. The existing debt of the County.

If the Town and County do not agree as to these items, the matter is settled by arbitration.

In making their award, the arbitrators must give credit to the Town for the share contributed by it in building roads and bridges outside of its limits. But when the roads and bridges are built within the Town it must be debited with their cost. The Town is also to be credited with its share in all County property except the Town's own roads and bridges.

When the Town and County come to an agreement, or in the case of dispute, when the arbitration award is made, a proclamation of the Lieutenant-Governor gives effect to the separation of the Town from the County.

The results of the separation are: 1—The Town is no longer represented in the County Council. 2.—The County Council can pass no by-law affecting the Town except in regard to the Court House, Gaol, or other County property in the town. 3.—The Town is not liable to the County except for the five items above described, and then as provided by the award.

With regard to the first four of these items, a new agreement or arbitration may be made after the lapse of five years. It may be made even sooner than this period, if the original agreement or award so states.

All property previously owned by the County, except town roads and bridges, remains the property of the County.

IV.—RE-UNION OF TOWN AND COUNTY.

After five years, a Town separated from a County may form a re-union with the County. But though the assent of a County is not required in the case of a separation, it is necessary for a re-union. The Town must be the first to pass the necessary by-law, with the assent of the electors, and then the by-law of the County must be passed within six months. The adjustment of their respective debts must take place, and in default of agreement, resort may be had to arbitration. No proclamation of the Lieutenant-Governor is needed, it would seem.

V.—TOWNSHIPS.

The Township is a municipality which, in regard to its formation depends upon its locality. In the older parts of the province, the townships are now for the most part, completely organized. In the case of a township which has been laid out in a county, but which has not been incorporated, it can receive its incorporation from a by-law of the County Council. If the township is not within any county, it can be incorporated by the Lieutenant-Governor, attaching it to an adjoining county.

When there is a Union of Townships, the junior Township can claim separate incorporation when it contains one hundred resident freeholders and householders on the last revised assessment roll. This incorporation takes effect on the first day of January after passing of a by-law in the previous year by the County Council.

It is the ordinary rule, as it will thus be seen, that a township should have at least one hundred resident freeholders and householders. However, if it has less than this number, but more than fifty, if two-thirds of such residents petition the County Council to separate the township from the Union, it lies with the County Council to perform the act of separation. The County Council cannot do this, however, unless it considers that from "streams or other natural obstructions" the township should not belong to the Union. The county council has also the power, on petition of two-thirds of the inhabitants of any township in the Union, to detach it from such Union and annex it to some other adjoining municipality.

When a dissolution of a Township Union takes place, the disposition of the property is, that the real property belongs to whatever township in which it is situated; thus each township will own whatever township hall is within its own limits. With regard to the other assets and the liabilities, the arrangement of them is provided for by agreement or by arbitration as in the case of separation of town from county. See page 22.

VI.—COUNTIES.

Counties are formed by proclamation of the Lieutenant-Governor. In the case of United Counties, the one in which the Court House and Gaol are situated, is the senior County.

The junior County may separate under the following method. If, by any statutory census, such as the Dominion census, or a census under the authority of a by-law of the United Counties, it appears the junior county contains 17,000 inhabitants or more, then the junior county may move for separation.

This is done by a majority of the Reeves and Deputy-Reeves of the junior county passing a resolution in the month of February in any year in favor of separation. Then, in the month of February of the following year, a majority of the Reeves and Deputy-Reeves are to send to the Lieutenant-Governor a petition for the separation. In such a case, if the Lieutenant-Governor deems the circumstances of the junior county such as to call for a separate establishment of courts and other county institutions, he may constitute the Reeves and Deputy-Reeves a Provisional Council. He appoints a time for the first meeting, names one of the members to preside, and determines which place shall be the County Town.

The member so named to preside, holds office until a provisional Warden is elected.

The council of the junior county is called a Provisional Council until the final separation takes place. The Provisional Council must first take steps to acquire land for and erect a Court House and Gaol. Not until these are erected can any arrangement between the senior and junior counties as to their joint assets and liabilities take place. This arrangement is effected by agreement, or in case of an agreement not being come to, then by arbitration. Of course the members of the Provisional Council, although they remain members of Union Council until the final separation, can not vote in the Union Council regarding any such agreement.

Whatever county is found to be in debt to the other after the arbitration is made, must pay interest at the rate of six per cent. from the time of dissolution.

After the agreement or arbitration, as the case may be, is concluded, the Ontario Government appoints the county officers who are to hold office in the junior county. These are a Sheriff, one or more Coroners, a clerk of the peace, a clerk of the county court, a Registrar and at least twelve Justices of the Peace.*

After these appointments are made, the final separation takes place through the issue of a proclamation of the Lieutenant-Governor. The separation takes place on the first of January next after the end of three months from the proclamation.

VII.—GENERAL MATTERS CONSEQUENT UPON THE FORMATION OF NEW CORPORATIONS.

There are certain matters which arise in consequence of the formation or alteration of corporations, as for instance, the formation of a village into a town, the separation of a town from a county, or the decreasing of the area of a village or town. Certain rules apply to all or most of these cases. These rules will here be treated to save repetition.

---

*The Judge is appointed by the Dominion Government.

If a village becomes incorporated, or an incorporated village becomes a town, or a town becomes a city, or townships and counties become separated, in all these cases the old by-laws remain in force until repealed or changed by the new corporation.

But no such by-laws can be repealed or altered unless the old council which passed them, could repeal or alter them. To explain the meaning of this, an instance may be given. If it happens that the old council had passed a by-law, sanctioned by the vote of the people, adopting the Canada Temperance Act, better known as the Scott Act, then this Scott Act by-law cannot be repealed except in the same way that the old council might have repealed it. To do this, a vote of the people must sanction the repeal, before the by-law can take effect.

The proceedings for such repeal cannot be taken any sooner than if there had been no change in the municipality.

Where the limits of a municipality, whether of a township, village or town, are extended, the territory added becomes at once subject to the existing by-laws of the Municipality, of which it has become a part. An exception to this rule is in regard to by-laws relating to roads and streets. The old by-laws relating to these will govern until the Municipality to which they are annexed repeals these old by-laws.

No change in a Municipality can affect creditors. Thus, as far as they are concerned, whatever may be the arrangement between a village becoming incorporated and the township of which it was a part, creditors can hold a village for the liabilities of the township when these liabilities were incurred before the separation of the village from the township. The same in regard to the separation of townships or counties from one another.

In the case of either a village, town or city receiving an addition of land, it shall pay to the township or county from which the tract has been taken such part of the debts of the township or county (if any) as may be just. If there is no agreement as to the amount of such debts within three months after the first meeting of the council of the municipality to which the addition has been made, then the matter is to be settled by arbitration.

When a county or township union is dissolved, the senior municipality shall issue debentures or other obligations for any part of any debt contracted by the union. These debentures shall recite the liability of the junior county therefor, and the junior county shall be liable as if they were debentures issued before the dissolution by the united counties.

The assessments for the year preceding the year in which the new corporation is formed shall belong to the old corporation. Special rates imposed by the old corporation for the payment of debts, which are required to be collected by the treasurer of the junior county, must be paid over by him to the treasurer of the senior county.

In the event of the sum paid over exceeding the just amount, the excess may be recovered.

Whenever there is a change in the formation of a municipal body, as for instance, when a village becomes a town, or in the case of separation, the council having authority previous to the change, continues its authority until the new council is organized. The officers also continue their offices, until they are dismissed, or successors appointed, and they have the same duties, powers and liabilities as before. It would be prudent, however, to have their sureties taken afresh. With regard to the officers of a senior county, there is no necessity of the sureties being renewed.

CHAPTER II.

THE MEMBERS OF MUNICIPAL COUNCILS—THEIR QUALIFICATIONS, DISQUALIFICATIONS AND EXEMPTIONS.

A municipal council is not the corporation itself. The corporation exists continually, but the council is elected from year to year. The council passes the by-laws of the corporation as the legislature passes the statutes of the country. In its own sphere, the council is more than the legislature is in its sphere; it is also an executive body, such as in the larger sphere, the Government is. A municipal council has only such powers as are expressly granted to it, and it cannot exceed them. For instance, a council has no power to donate as a gift a certain sum of money such as for a banquet. We will now discuss how in the several kinds of municipalities, councils are composed.

COMPOSITION OF MUNICIPAL COUNCILS.

In Counties, the council is composed of the Reeves and Deputy-Reeves of Townships and of Towns not separated from the County. The Warden who is elected from among either the Reeves or Deputy-Reeves is the head of the County Council.

Before a Reeve or Deputy-Reeve takes his seat in the County Council he must file with the County clerk, a certificate from the clerk of his own municipality in a form like the following:—

I, A. B , of   , Clerk of the Corporation of the Township (Town or Village *as the case may be*) of   , in the County of   , do hereby under my hand and the seal of the said Corporation certify that C. D., of   , Esquire was duly elected Reeve (*or Deputy Reeve, as the case may be*) of the said Township (Town or Village *as the case may be*) and has made and subscribed the declarations of office and qualification as such Reeve, (*or Deputy-Reeve as the case may be*). Given under my hand and the seal of the said Corporation of   , at   , in the said Township (Town *or* Village, *as the case may be*) this   day of   , A. D. 18 .

A. B.,

Township (Town *or* Village) Clerk.

Each Deputy-Reeve, besides filing the above certificate, must also file another from the clerk of his own municipality as follows:—

I, A. B., of   , *Gentleman*, Clerk of the Township (Town *or* Village, *as the case may be*) of   , in the County of   , do hereby declare and affirm as follows:—

(1.) That I am the person having the legal custody of the last revised assessment roll for the said Township (Town *or* Village, *as the case may be*).

(2.) That there appear upon the said roll the names of at least   hundred (500 *for each Deputy-Reeve*) freeholders and householders in the said Township (Town or Village *as the case may be*) possessing the same property qualification as voters.

(3.) That no alteration reducing the limits of the said Municipality, and the number of persons possessing the same property qualification as voters below   hundred (500 *for each Deputy-Reeve*) has taken place since the said roll was last revised.

A. B.

In Cities, The Council is composed of the Mayor,

who is the head, and three Aldermen for each Ward.

In Towns, the Council is composed of the Mayor, who is the head, and three Councillors for each Ward, where the Wards are less than five. If there are five or more Wards there are two Councillors for each Ward. Thus a Town with only four Wards has more Councillors (12) than a Town with five Wards, which will have only ten Councillors.*

In case the Town is not separated from the County it has a Reeve and also Deputy-Reeves, there being a Deputy-Reeve for each 500 inhabitants *possessing the same qualification as voters*. Among these 500 are to be calculated such freeholders and householders who, although they are such, are yet not voters.

In Villages the Council is composed of a Reeve, who is the head, and four Councillors. If the Village has the names of 500 freeholders and householders on the last revised assessment roll, *possessing the same qualification as voters* (see preceding paragraph), then the Council is composed of a Reeve, Deputy-Reeve and three Councillors. For every additional 500 the village is entitled to another Deputy-Reeve, who takes the place of a Councillor.

In Townships, the composition of the Council is the same as just described in regard to villages. But, as has been mentioned in a preceding page, a Township may be divided into wards, while a Village

---

*A Town with less than five Wards may now reduce the Councillors for each Ward to two. This is done by a petition of at least 100 electors to the Council, who then pass a by-law, which by-law must be sanctioned by a vote of the electors. Any time after two annual elections the same proceedings may be taken to repeal the change and restore the three Councillors.

can not be so divided. Where, therefore, there are wards in a Township, Councillors are elected for the respective wards. But there cannot be an increase of wards so as to increase the number of Councillors.

In Provisional Corporations (see page 25) the Reeves and Deputy-Reeves of the municipalities within a Junior County for which a Provisional Council is established shall by virtue of their local tenure of office as Reeves, Councillors, etc., be the members of the Provisional Council.

QUALIFICATIONS.

Having explained how the Councils in the several municipalities are composed, we will now speak of the qualification which the members must possess.

Firstly.—Every member of the Council of any municipality must answer to the following requirements for his office.

1. He must reside within the municipality or within two miles thereof.

2. He must be a natural born or naturalized British subject.*

3. Must be a male of the full age of twenty-one years.

4. Must not come within the list of persons disqualified, who are mentioned hereafter under the head of "Disqualifications."

These are the general requisites for every member of a Council, whether Mayor, Alderman, Reeve,

---

*As to who are British subjects a very long chapter might be written, to explain under various circumstances which arise, who is a subject and who an alien. The rules of international law have changed somewhat of late years in regard to this matter.

Deputy-Reeve or Councillor. Besides these there is a property qualification prescribed as follows :—

In Villages.—Freehold to $600, or leasehold to $1,200.

In Towns.—Freehold to $800, or leasehold to $1,600.

In Cities.—Freehold to $1,500, or leasehold to $3,000.

In Townships.—Freehold to $400, or leasehold to $800.

And where the qualification is partly freehold and partly leasehold, it can be taken proportionately.

The property may be held in a member's own right, or in that of his wife, so as to qualify him.

It may be property of which he has a deed, or it is sufficient if he is entitled to it in other ways, without actually having the deed in his name.

It must be worth the required amount over and above all charges, liens and encumbrances, as for instance, mortgages and executions.

The assessment roll determines what is the value of the property. But this is necessarily otherwise in new Townships, for which there has been no assessment roll.

With regard to the leasehold qualification it must be at least a tenancy for a year.

DISQUALIFICATIONS.

The following persons can not be members of any municipal council :—

- Judges of Courts of Civil Jurisdiction.
- Gaolers or Keepers of Houses of Correction.
- Sheriffs, Deputy-Sheriffs and Sheriff's bailiffs.
- High Bailiff or Chief Constable of any City or

Town.
　Assessors of *any* Municipality.
　Collectors　　"　　　　"
　Treasurers　　"　　　　"
　Clerks　　　　"　　　　"
　Bailiffs of Division Courts.
　County Crown Attorneys.
　Registrars.
　Deputy Clerks of the Crown.
　Clerks of the County Court.
　Clerks of the Peace.
　Inn Keepers, Saloon Keepers, or Shop Keepers licensed to sell spirituous liquors by retail.
　License Commissioners, and Inspectors of Licenses.
　Police Magistrates, and
　Persons having by themselves or partners an interest in any contract with or on behalf of the Corporation.

These last named persons (as indeed to a large extent the others) are disqualified so as to guard against the abuse or mischief of a councillor's private interest conflicting with his duty to the public. As instances of persons who have been taken by the courts to come within this class, may be mentioned the following:—A wood and coal dealer who had tendered for the supply of wood and coal; a baker who had contracted to supply bread to the gaol; a surety for the corporation treasurer; a person who contracted with the corporation to maintain a bridge for forty years, etc., etc.

It matters not whether the contract is in the name of the person himself, or in that of another, as long as the person is really the contractor.

The best opinion seems to be that where the work is completed under a contract and nothing remains but payment, the contractor would not be disqualified.

However, if there is any unsettled dispute arising out of the contract (as to the amount due, for instance) though the contract is actually completed, yet the contractor would be disqualified.

If a man is an agent only of a person having a contract with the corporation he is qualified.

But a partner of a person having a contract, it will be observed, is disqualified.

It is considered by good authority that a subcontractor would not be disqualified.

The disqualification relates to the date of the election, not merely to the time of acceptance of office; it might go so far back as nomination day. So it would be prudent that a person having a contract should be free from it before being nominated.

If the election is by acclamation, the objection to the party being disqualified by reason of a contract at the time of the election can not afterwards be taken.

If a member of a Council is also a shareholder in a company, though he is qualified in other respects, he can not vote on any question affecting the company. Thus, where four out of five members in the Council of the then village (now the town) of Almonte were also shareholders of a certain company, and voted a bonus to the company, which bonus was ratified by the ratepayers, the by-law was set aside by the Court.

EXEMPTIONS.

The preceding paragraphs relate to persons who are disqualified. There are also others who, *although qualified*, may, if they choose, claim to be exempted. The ordinary rule is that people who are qualified must serve, if elected. The following is a list of those who may exercise, at their option, the right to refuse being elected. :

Members of the Legislature, Senate or House of Commons.

Persons in the Civil Service.

Judges, who are not disqualified as before mentioned.*

Coroners.

Persons in Priests' orders, Clergymen and Ministers of the Gospel of every denomination.

Barristers, or students at law.

Attorneys and Solicitors in actual practice.

All officers of Courts of Justice.

Physicians and Surgeons.

Professors, Masters, Teachers and other members of any University, College or School in Ontario, and all officers and servants thereof.

Millers.

Firemen belonging to an authorized Fire Company.†

---

*The meaning of this is that there are certain Judges who are absolutely disqualified. There are others who are not, but they may claim exemption.

†Even after they cease to be Firemen, if they have served seven years, they are exempt, also from personal statute labor and from serving as Jurors or Constables.

CHAPTER III.

MUNICIPAL ELECTIONS.

Nominations.

The nominations for members of Councils take place on the last Monday in December of each year.

If the last Monday in December happens to be Christmas Day, the nomination takes place on the preceding Friday instead.

The County Council may by a by-law passed before the 1st July in any year provide that the nomination shall be on the last Monday but one in December. This by-law must be sent by the County Clerk to the Township Clerks. It is only the nomition day that can be so changed, and such changes can affect Townships only.

The meetings of electors for nomination take place at the following hours of the day.

For Mayors in Cities, and for Mayors, Reeves and Deputy-Reeves in Towns—at ten o'clock, a. m.

For Aldermen in Cities, Councillors in Towns, Reeves, Deputy-Reeves and Councillors in such Townships as have no Wards, and in Villages—at noon.

For townships divided into wards, the nomination for Reeve at ten o'clock a.m. and Councillors at noon.

The place for holding nominations for Mayors of cities and towns, and Reeves and Deputy Reeves of towns is fixed at the city or town hall. If another place were taken, it would likely void the election, as happened once in New Brunswick, though there is no reported case of the kind in this province.

The places for other nominations are fixed by the by-laws of the municipalities.

The presiding officer at nomination of Mayors, Reeves and Deputy-Reeves in Towns is the Clerk. In the case of his absence the Council shall appoint a person to preside in his place. Whoever presides is to be the Returning Officer.

In regard to municipalities where there are Wards and polling subdivisions, the places of nomination, the Returning Officers, the polling places, and the Deputy Returning Officer are appointed from time to time by by-laws. A resolution of the Council instead of a regular by-law will not suffice for these purposes.

The Clerk of the Township is the Returning Officer for the whole municipality.

The Returning Officer appointed for Wards presides at nomination meetings.

In Townships where there are no Wards and in villages, the Clerk is the Returning officer.

Every returning officer whose duty it is to preside at nomination meetings must give at least six days notice of the meeting.

Whenever a Returning Officer is not present at a nomination meeting, the meeting must elect a chairman. If there is no presiding officer, the nominations would most likely be void.

If, after the lapse of an hour from the time fixed for holding the meeting there happens to be only one candidate for a particular office nominated, the Clerk, Returning Officer. or Chairman, is the case may be, shall declare such candidate elected for the office.

When two or more candidates are nominated, then, in case a poll is demanded by them or by an elector, the Clerk, Returning Officer, or Chairman shall adjourn the proceedings until the first Monday in January, when the polls are to be opened from nine a.m. until five p.m. and no longer.

Every candidate must be proposed and seconded.

At the nomination meeting a candidate may resign with the consent of his proposer and seconder.

If one person is nominated for two or more offices, he should choose which office he will stand for; if he does not make his choice, then he is a candidate only for the office for which he was first nominated.

The Clerk, or other Returning Officer, or Chairman must, on the day following nomination day, put up in the Clerk's office the names of the persons proposed for the several offices.

RULES AS TO TIME AND PLACE OF ELECTION.

On the first Monday in January, the elections for every municipality take place, excepting, of course, where elections have been by acclamation.

The persons elected, hold office until their successors are sworn into office and the following year's Council is organized.

In the following cases :—

Where a new township is incorporated,

Where a junior township is separated from a union.

In a newly incorporated village,

When a village becomes a town,

When a town becomes a city,

Where an additional tract of land is added to a village, town or city,

Or, in case of a new division into wards of a town or city,

there must be a lapse of three months between the time when the change was proclaimed by the Lieutenant-Governor, or the by-law of the County Council relating thereto was passed, (as the case may be), and the time of election. If the first Monday in January comes before the end of any such three months, the change does not go into effect until the following year. As long as the three months have elapsed before the first Monday in January, elections by acclamation on nomination day (*i. e.* the last Monday in December) are valid, though the three months are not complete on nomination day.

The Council of each municipality by by-law appoint the place or places for holding the ensuing municipal elections. In the event of their not doing so, then in cities, towns and villages the election takes place where it was held the previous year. In townships, the election takes place when no by-law is passed, where the last meeting of the Council was held.

The County Council appoints the place of first election in junior Townships after separation. This is done by by-law passed before the 31st October. The by-law should appoint a Returning Officer and also otherwise provide for the due holding of the election according to law.

When a separation of union townships takes place

the existing divisions into wards cease in both townships. Each of the separated townships may afterwards be divided into wards.

The manner in which a township is divided into wards is by a petition of the majority of the qualified electors on the last revised assessment roll to the Township Council. The Council is bound within one month after receiving the petition to pass the by-law. In the same way, by petition and by-law, the wards may be abolished.

The number of electors in each ward should be as nearly equal as may be.

The number of wards must be four. Each ward elects a Councillor, and the Councillors of the wards elect the Deputy-Reeves from among themselves. This (excepting the Warden of the county) is the only exception to the general rule that all the members of any Municipal Council are elected directly by the body of the electors. Even in the case of the Warden and the Deputy-Reeves of townships divided into wards, these are elected in the first place by the people to the inferior office. Before 1866, Mayors, Reeves and Deputy-Reeves were elected by the Council, but this is now abolished except in Townships divided into wards where the Councillors elect the Deputy-Reeves, as before mentioned.

Every election must be held within the limits of the municipality to which it relates.

No election of Township Councillors shall be held within any city, town or village.

No election shall be held in a tavern or place licensed to sell liquor.

Who are Qualified to Vote?

Electors must be males of the full age of twenty-one years, British subjects by birth or naturalization, and be rated (on the last revised assessment roll upon which the voters' list used at the election is based) for real property either in their own right or in the right of their wives or for income as follows:—

1st. Freeholders or husbands of freeholders whether residents or not.*

2nd. Householders who are, for one month before and at the date of the election residents. This includes residents whose wives are householders or tenants.

3rd. Income voters, rated for $400 income, who are residents at the election, and continuously so resided since the completion of the last revised assessment roll. Their income must be derived from "some trade, office, calling or profession." This would not appear to cover incomes derived from investments or other sources than those just mentioned.

4th. Farmers' sons. The qualification of farmers' sons will be treated a little further on.

Amount of property required.—As to the value of the property, *electors* who qualify either as freeholders or householders are required to be rated as follows:—In townships—$100; in incorporated villages—$200; in towns—$300; in cities, $400.

The property may be partly freehold and partly leasehold.

---

*Every occupant of a separate portion of a house, such portion having a distinct communication with a public road or street by an outer door is deemed to be a householder.

Who are residents,—The residence of a person is where his home is situated, or where his family live. A man cannot, within the meaning of our municipal laws, be said to be resident within two municipalities. A case is reported where a man had a dwelling house in Bowmanville, besides having a saw mill, and being postmaster in the township of Cartwright; he occasionally visited the latter place and boarded with one of his employees there. It was decided by the Court that after voting in Bowmanville, he could not vote in Cartwright. When a man has an actual residence in a place, occasional absence will not prevent his being considered a resident.

Farmers' sons,—The qualification of farmers' sons needs special mention. A farmer's son must be twelve months a resident prior to the return of the assessment roll by the Assessor. If the farm is rated only for enough to give the father a vote, then the son will have none. According as it is rated sufficient, so will so many sons, according to the value of the farm, (if divided equally between them) beginning with the eldest son, have a right to vote.

A farmer's son has a right to vote, where a mother owns the property.

Absence from time to time during the twelve months will not disqualify a farmer's son, provided that taken altogether the times do not exceed four months.

The farm must be twenty acres, and occupied by the father or mother, who must be the owner. The father may be a step-father, but it does not appear that the term mother, would include step-mother.

Tax defaulters,—If the municipality passes a by-law to disqualify electors who have not paid taxes before the 14th December, then any such persons have no vote. The list, if returned by the Collector to the Treasurer, is verified by the oath of the Treasurer; if it is not so returned, then by the oath of the Collector himself.

The list contains income tax defaulters, and also, in case the municipality has passed such a by-law as has just been spoken of, also the defaulters in property taxes. It will be observed that with or without such a by-law an income voter must have paid his tax. A property voter is not disqualified unless the required by-law of the municipality to disqualify such voters has been passed.

Voters' list final.—An elector must be named on the voters' list to entitle him to vote, and the defaulters' list is the guide as to whether he is disqualified in respect to non-payment of taxes.

A mis-spelling of a voter's name does not prevent his voting. Even a wrong Christian name, such as "Joseph" for "James" does not disentitle a voter, and it has been held that "Thomas Anderson" has a right to vote when he was described as "Thomas Sanderson." The main question is, whether the voter is the identical person on the list.

Voters in New Municipalities.—In the case of a new municipality when there is no separate assessment roll, at the first election the voters' qualification must of necessity be arrived at, without the aid of a roll.

Voters in case of addition of new territory.—Where new territory is added to a city, town or village, or a newly made city, town or village is formed, with new territory added to the old municipality, then the persons who before the changed state of affairs would be qualified to vote, can vote. This refers to an election taking place before the regular voters' list is made out.

Owners and occupants.—Where both an owner and occupant are *severally* rated for property, both shall be deemed to be rated, so as to qualify them.

Joint owners and occupants.—Where two or more own property jointly, or occupy it jointly, then so that both can be qualified the property must be rated at such an amount as, if it were equally divided, it would give a qualification to each.

THE RETURNING OFFICERS AND DEPUTY-RETURNING OFFICERS:

The Clerk of the municipality is the Returning Officer for the whole municipality. Where the election is to be by wards or polling subdivisions, the Returning Officers for each ward who receive the nominations, and the Deputy-Returning Officers who preside at the polling-places are appointed by by-law of the Council. These latter must make their returns to the Clerk.

Where there are no wards, the clerk is the Returning Officer both for nomination and for polling.

In the following cases—1. Where the Returning Officer or Deputy-Returning Officer has died. 2. Or when he does not attend within an hour after the time appointed. 3. Or, in case no Returning Officer or Deputy-Returning Officer has been appointed,—the electors present at the place for holding the nomination or poll may choose from amongst themselves a Returning or Deputy-Returning Officer.

A Returning or Deputy-Returning Officer is a Conservator of the peace in the city or county in which the election is held. Either he or a Justice of the Peace, may summarily try and punish by fine or imprisonment, or both, or may imprison or bind over to keep the peace, or bind over for trial, any riotous or disorderly person who assaults, beats, molests or threatens any voter, coming to, remaining at, or going from the election or voting.

Constables and persons present must assist the Officer or a Justice of the Peace. The Returning Officer or Deputy Returning Officer has also the power to appoint special constables.

The present Chief Justice of the Common Pleas, some years ago made the following remarks in a case, "A Returning Officer so appointed should not be a partizan. It is the duty of a Returning Officer to stand indifferent between the contending parties; to have no interest to serve for either, or for himself; to approach his duty with a simple desire to do strict justice; to be ready and willing to give reasonable information as to the state of his proceedings; to conceal nothing; to evade no proper enquiry; to mislead no one by silence, or exhibit anything calculated to deceive; and he ought not to make a pretence of strictly following the letter of the law, to defeat it."

OATHS.

The Returning or Deputy-Returning Officer may administer oaths or affirmations to voters according to the forms in the Municipal Act. These forms relate to freeholders, householders, income voters and farmers' sons.

The form of a Freeholder's Oath is as follows:—

You swear (*or* solemnly affirm) that you are the person named or purporting to be named, in the list (*or* supplementary list) of voters now shewn to you (*shewing the list to the voter*);

That you are a freeholder in your own right (*or* right of your wife, *as the case may require*);

That you are a natural born citizen (*or* naturalized) subject of Her Majesty, and of the full age of twenty-one years;

(*In the case of Municipalities not divided into Wards.*) That you have not voted before at this election, either at this or any other polling place.

(*In the case of Municipalities divided into Wards.*) That you have not voted before at this election, either at this or any other polling place in this Ward and (*if the elector is tendering his vote for Mayor, Reeve or Deputy-Reeve*) that you have not voted before or elsewhere in this Municipality at this election for Mayor (Reeve or Deputy Reeve *as the case may be*);

That you have not directly or indirectly received any reward or gift, nor do you expect to receive any, for the vote which you tender at this election;

That you have not received anything, nor has anything been promised to you, directly or indirectly, either to induce you to vote at this election, or for loss of time, travelling expenses, hire of team, or any other service connected with this election;

And that you have not directly or indirectly paid or promised anything to any person either to induce him to vote or refrain from voting at this election;

So help you God.

(*In the case of a new Municipality in which there has not been any assessment roll, then instead of referring to the list of voters, the person offering to vote may be required to state in the oath the property in respect of which he claims to vote.*)

The form of a householder's oath is as follows:—

You swear (*or* solemnly affirm) that you are the person named or purporting to be named in the list (*or* suplementary list) of voters now shewn to you (*shewing the list to the voter*);

That on the   day of   18   (*the day certified by the Clerk of the Municipality as the date of the return, or of the final revision and correction, of the assessment roll upon which the voters' list used at the election is based*) you were actually, truly and in good faith, possessed to your own use and benefit as tenant or occupant, of the real estate in respect of which your name is entered on the said list;

That you are (or your wife is) a householder or tenant within this Municipality;

That you have been resident within this Municipality for one month next before this election;

That you are a natural born (or naturalized) subject of Her Majesty, and of the full age of twenty-one years;

(*In the case of Municipalities not divided into Wards.*) That you have not voted before at this election, either at this or any other polling place.

(*In the case of Municipalities divided into Wards.*) That you have not voted before at this election, either at this or any other polling place in this Ward and (*if the elector is tendering his vote for Mayor, Reeve or Deputy-Reeve*) that you have not voted before or elsewhere in this Municipality at this election for Mayor (Reeve or Deputy Reeve *as the case may be*);

That you have not directly or indirectly received any reward or gift, nor do you expect to receive any, for the vote which you tender at this election;

That you have not received anything, nor has anything been promised to you, directly or indirectly, either to induce you to vote at this election, or for loss of time, travelling expenses, hire of team, or any other service connected with this election;

And that you have not directly or indirectly paid or promised anything to any person either to induce him to vote or refrain from voting at this election;

So help you God.

(*In the case of a new Municipality in which there has not been any assessment roll, then instead of swearing to residence for one month next before the election, and referring to the list of voters, the person offering to vote may be required to state in the oath the property in respect of which he claims to vote, and that he is a resident of such Municipality.)*

The form of an Income Voter's Oath is as follows:—

You swear (*or* solemnly affirm) that you are the person named or purporting to be named, by the name of   on the list (*or* supplementary list) of voters now shewn to you (*shewing the list to voter*);

That on the   day of   18   (*the day certified by the Clerk of the Municipality as the date of the final revision and correction of the assessment roll upon which the voters' list used at the election is based*), you were and thenceforward have been continuously, and still are, a resident of this Township (City, Town *or* Village, *as the case may be*);

That at the said date, and for twelve months previously, you were in receipt of an income from your trade (office, calling *or* profession, *as the case may be*) of a sum not less than $400;

That you are a subject of Her Majesty by birth (*or* naturalization, *as the case may be*); and are of the full age of twenty-one years;

(*In the case of Municipalities not divided into Wards.*) That you have not voted before at this election, either at this or any other polling place;

(*In the case of Municipalities divided into Wards.*) That you have not voted before at this election, either at this or any other polling place in this Ward, and (*if the elector is tendering his vote for Mayor, Reeve or Deputy-Reeve*) that you have not voted before or elsewhere in this Municipality at this election for Mayor (Reeve *or* Deputy-Reeve, *as the case may be*);

That you have not received anything, nor has anything been promised you, either directly or indirectly, either to induce you to vote at this election, or for loss of time, travelling expenses, hire of team, or any other service connected with this election;

And that you have not directly or indirectly, paid or promised anything to any person, either to induce him to

vote or refrain from voting at this election:
So help you God.

The form of a Farmers Son's oath is as follows:—

You swear (*or solemnly affirm*) that you are the person named or purporting to be named by the name of
        , in the list (*or supplementary list*) of voters now shewn to you (*shewing the list to the voter*);

That on the   day of   , 18   (*the day certified by the Clerk of the municipality, as the date of the return, or of the final revision and correction of the assessment roll upon which the voters' list used at the election is based, as the case requires*, A.B. (*naming him or her*), was actually, truly, and in good faith possessed to his (*or her*) own use and benefit as owner, as you verily believe, of the real estate in respect of which your name is so as aforesaid entered on said list of voters;

That you are a son of the said A.B.;

That you resided on the said property for twelve months next before the said day, not having been absent during that period, except temporarily, and not more than four months in all:

That you are still a resident of this Municipality, and entitled to vote at this election;

That you are a subject of Her Majesty by birth (*or naturalization as the case may be*); and are of the full age of twenty-one years;

(*In the case of municipalities not divided into Wards.*) That you have not voted before at this election, either at this or any other polling place;

(*In the case of municipalities divided into Wards.*) That you have not voted before at this election, either at this or any other polling-place in this Ward, and (*if the elector is tendering his vote for Mayor, Reeve or Deputy-Reeve*) that you have not voted before or elsewhere in this Municipality at this election for Mayor, (Reeve, *or* Deputy-Reeve *as the case may be*);

That you have not received anything, nor has anything been promised you directly or indirectly either to induce you to vote at this election, or for loss of time, travelling expenses, hire of team, or any other service connected with this election;

And that you have not directly or indirectly paid or promised anything to any person either to induce him to vote or refrain from voting at this election:

So help you God.

Any candidate or his authorized agent may insist on the oath being administered.

No enquiries shall be made of any voter except with respect to the facts specified in such oaths or affirmations.

An improper refusal to take a vote will render a Returning or Deputy-Returning Officer liable to an action for damages at the instance of the voter.

THE POLLING.

It is the duty of the clerk to provide ballot boxes at the expense of the municipality. A penalty of $100 for every ballot box which he fails to provide is imposed on him. It is his duty to provide these ballot boxes two days at least before the polling day. If he fails to do so a Deputy-Returning Officer may procure the necessary ballot box, sign an order on the Treasurer for the cost, and the Treasurer must thereupon pay the Deputy-Returning Officer for the same.

Ballot papers must also be procured by the clerk at the expense of the municipality. These should be printed alphabetically in the order of surnames of the candidates; if there are candidates with the same surname, then in the order of their other name.

Where a Mayor, Reeve, or Deputy-Reeves are to be elected at the same time with Aldermen or

Councillors, then there must be one set of ballot papers for the offices gereral to the whole municipality and another for the ward aldermen or councillors, as the case may be. This rule does not apply to townships which are not divided into wards.

There must be a compartment in the polling place in which the voters can mark their votes, secured from observation. The returning officer must also post up before the opening of the poll, the "printed directions to voters" which are given in the schedule B at the end of the Municipal Act. Copies must be posted up in every compartment of the polling place, and also outside it. If he does not get them from the Clerk, (whose duty it is to procure them for him) until after the opening of the poll, then he must put them up as soon as he gets them.

These printed directions must be in "conspicuous characters."

Voters' Lists.—The voters' lists to be used at an election shall be the first and second parts of the last list of voters certified by the Judge and transmitted by him to the Clerk of the Peace.

But where a new municipality has an election for the first time, and has no separate assessment roll, the clerk provides each deputy-returning officer with a blank poll book, in the form prescribed by the Municipal Act of 1883, sec. 128. The persons who tender their votes are entered upon such book and if requested by any candidate or voter, the deputy-returning officer or sworn poll clerk must enter opposite each name the property on which the person claims to vote.

Besides the regular voters' list, there is also a supplementary voters' list in the case of new territory being added to the city, town or village, or where a town or village with additions respectively becomes a city or town. In these cases the clerk forms the supplementary lists just spoken of by putting in it the names of persons who would be voters, in case the territory had not been added, but remained in the municipality of which it had formerly been a portion.

Where there is no voters' list filed with the Clerk of the Peace or certified by the County Judge, the Clerk of the Municipality shall, before the poll is opened prepare a list for each ward or polling subdivision of all male persons entitled by the last revised assessment roll attested in writing under his hand by his solemn declaration. This list is to be delivered to the deputy-returning officer before the poll is opened. Income voters and property voters disqualified as mentioned on page 45 are to be left out of such list. A list of such defaulters as well as the voters' list must be delivered by the Clerk to deputy-returning officers. Such lists are to be acted upon by the deputy-returning officers.

The Clerk must also give to the deputy-returning officer a certificate of the dates, 1st, of the return; 2ndly, of the final revision of the assessment roll. Any person may demand such certificate on payment of 25 cents. A Clerk by refusing it incurs the penalty of $200.

Persons can vote only once for Mayor, Reeve, or Deputy-Reeves; and for Aldermen or Councillors, property voters can vote in each ward in which they are qualified. A person voting twice for Mayor, etc., incurs a penalty of $50 and forfeits his right to vote or be a candidate at the next annual elections.

Deputy-returning officers, poll clerks and agents may vote where they are stationed, on a certificate from the clerk—the certificate stating the property in any other polling sub-division or ward where they are entitled to vote. Such certificate must be attached by the deputy-returning officer to the voters' list. This provision does not apply to elections for Aldermen or Councillors, so as to allow any such person to vote in one ward for Aldermen or Councillors in another ward. But they may vote in a different polling sub-division of the same ward.

Immediately before the poll is commenced, the Deputy-Returning Officer shall shew the ballot box to such persons as are present in the polling place, so that they may see that it is empty. It is then locked and sealed by him, so that it cannot be opened without breaking the seal.

The Deputy-Returning Officer, after ascertaining that the name of the voter is on the list, shall record it, as well as his residence and legal addition. By "legal addition" is meant the occupation, profession, trade, etc., of a person.

The voter is to be marked on the list, "sworn," "affirmed," "refused to be sworn" or "refused to affirm," as the case may be. If he is objected to by a candidate or agent, he is to be marked on the list with the words "objected to," and after these words the name of the candidate on whose behalf he is objected to.

After making the necessary entries of name, etc.,

just mentioned, the deputy-returning officer, after signing his name or initials on the ballot paper, delivers it to the voter. If requested, he must explain or get his poll clerk to explain to a voter the mode of voting.

After a voter has marked his ballot and returns it to the Deputy-Returning Officer the latter verifies his initials (so as to satisfy himself that it is the same ballot as delivered to the voter.)

The form of voting, instructing illiterate voters, and the general details of balloting are so well known, that it would be superfluous to go into them here. The leading principle of voting by ballot is, of course, secrecy. The following brief rules in addition to those already explained, may be given.

Spoiled ballot papers, when returned by a voter, are to be marked "cancelled," by the deputy returning officer, and a new ballot is to be given to such voter. All ballot papers must be returned by the deputy-returning officer.

No person is entitled or permitted to be present in the polling place, other than the officers, candidates, clerks or agents of candidates, and such voter as is engaged in voting. A candidate may have two agents besides himself in a polling place.

A constable may be called in for the purpose of maintaining order or preserving the public peace, or to remove persons contravening the election law.

After the poll is closed, the deputy-returning officer must immediately, in the presence of the poll clerk (if any) and "such of the candidates or their agents as may then be present," open the box and proceed to count the ballots.

The following ballots are not to be counted :—
Those without the name or initials of the deputy returning officer on the back; those on which more votes are given than the elector is entitled to give, and thirdly, those on which anything except the name or initials of the deputy returning officer is written or marked, by which the voter can be identified.

With regard to those ballots, where votes are given for more candidates than a voter is entitled to vote for, they are good as to any other votes for another office properly marked on such ballots.

The deputy returning officer must take a note of any objections to ballot papers made by a candidate or agent, or any elector entitled to be present. The way of noting such objections is to number them, and then place a corresponding number on the back of the ballot paper. Such number on the ballot paper is to be initialed by the deputy returning officer.

He shall endorse the ballots rejected by him with the word "rejected," and if his decision is objected to, he shall endorse also the words, "rejection objected to."

After counting the ballots, he must make up a written statement in words as well as in figures under the following heads:—

(a.) Name or Number of Ward or polling subdivision and of the Municipality, and the date of the election.

(b.) Number of votes for each candidate.

(c.) Rejected ballot papers.

Such statement must be signed by the deputy returning officer, the poll clerk (if any) and such of the candidates or agents present as desire to sign it.

A deputy returning officer must give a certificate, if requested, to the persons authorized to attend at his polling place, of the following particulars:—1. Number of votes for each candidate, and,—2. The number of rejected ballot papers. Any simple form of certificate, as long as it embodies these statements, will suffice.

The deputy returning officer must also certify under his signature on the voters' list itself, the total number of voters who have voted. This must be done in full words, not figures.

He must also, in the presence of the agents of the candidates, make up into separate packets, sealed with his own seal, the following papers:

1. The statement of votes given for each candidate and of the rejected ballot papers.*
2. The used ballot papers which have not been objected to and have been counted.
3. The ballot papers which have been objected to, but which have been counted by him.
4. The rejected ballot papers.
5. The spoiled ballot papers.
6. The unused ballot papers.
7. A statement of the number of voters whose votes are marked by the deputy returning officer under the heads, "Physical incapacity" and "Unable to read," with the declarations of inability; and the notes taken of objections made to ballot papers found in the ballot box.

---

*See preceding page as to this statement.

The agents of the candidates may, if they desire it, seal the packets. The deputy returning officer is to mark on each one what it contains, also the date of the day of the election, the name of the deputy returning officer and the ward or polling sub-division and municipality.

When the clerk of the municipality is not himself the deputy returning officer, the deputy returning officer shall forthwith deliver such packets personally to the clerk.

Before returning the voters' list to the clerk, the deputy returning officer shall make and subscribe, either before the clerk or a Justice of the Peace, an oath which must be annexed to the voters' list. The following is the form of the oath:—

I, C. D., the undersigned Deputy Returning officer for polling sub-division No.   , of the City (*or as the case may be*) of   , in the County of   , do solemnly swear (*or if he is a person permitted by law to affirm, do solemnly affirm*) that to the best of my knowledge the annexed voters' list used in and for the said polling sub-division No.   , of the said City (*or as the case may be*), was so used in the manner prescribed by law and that the entries required by law to be made therein were correctly made.

     (Signed)   C. D.
Sworn (*or* affirmed) before me at   , this day of   , A. D., 18

    (Signed) X Y.,
      Justice of the Peace.
    Or, A. B.,
    Clerk of Municipality of

If he is unable to do so, owing to illness or any other cause, another person chosen by him may deliver them. Outside the cover of each of the packets, the name of such person is to be mentioned, and the deputy returning officer is to take a receipt from such person. The ballot box is also to be returned to the clerk.

The deputy returning officer must also return with the packets a statement called the "Ballot Paper Account." This account must show the number of ballot papers entrusted to him and account for them under the following heads:—1. Counted; 2. Rejected; 3. Unused; 4. Spoiled; 5. Ballot papers given to voters who afterwards returned the same, declining to vote; and 6. Ballot papers taken from the polling place.

In case there is a dispute as to the result, when a written statement as to the votes is made by the deputy returning officer, the packages of ballot papers shall be broken open by the clerk of the municipality at an hour and place appointed on the day succeeding the polling day. This is done in the presence of the deputy returning officer and such of the candidates or their agents as may be present. If the distance necessary to be travelled is such that the appointed place can not be reached on the day following the poll, then a reasonable time (but no more) is allowed for the purpose of coming. before the clerk of the municipality.

The clerk shall, after examining the ballot papers, finally determine the matter in dispute and sign the written statement. He then must securely seal up, in the presence of all, the ballot papers in their several packages as before.

After the return of ballot papers and statements, the clerk is required to cast up from the *statements* the number of votes for each candidate, and he is to publicly declare, on the day following the receipt of the ballot papers and statements, the candidate or candidates having the highest number of votes, to be elected. This is done at the Town Hall, or if there is no Town Hall, then at some other public place. The clerk must also post up in some conspicuous place a statement showing the number of votes for each candidate.

The clerk has a casting vote in the event of a tie. Any person acting instead of the clerk, as mentioned on page 39, has in such a case a casting vote. This is the only occasion on which a clerk has the right to vote at a municipal election.

If by reason of a riot or other emergency an election is not commenced on the proper day, or is interrupted after being commenced, then the election is to be resumed on the following day at 10 o'clock a. m., and continue from day to day, *if necessary*, "until the poll has been opened without interruption and with free access to voters, for twelve hours in all, or thereabouts." This is in order that all electors may have a fair opportunity to vote.

If election is prevented for four days the poll book is to be returned and a new election ordered under the warrant of the head of the municipality.

A clerk has nothing to do in regard to deciding as to the qualification of a candidate. This remains for the courts to adjudicate upon.

The Clerk must retain all ballot papers for one month, and then unless otherwise ordered by a Court or Judge, he must destroy them in the presence of two witnesses, who have to make a declaration as to their being destroyed. The following may be given as a form of declaration:—

We, A. B. and C. D., of the town (*or as the case may be*) of   in the County of   , hereby declare that we were personally present and did witness the ballot papers received by E. F., the Clerk of this municipality in the elections for Mayor, Reeve, Deputy-Reeves and Councillors for the present year in this town (*or as the case may be*) destroyed by him.

Dated this   day of   A.D. 18 .

Declared before me at
this   day of   A.D. 18 . } A. B.
      G. H.,
      Mayor of   } C. D.
      (*or as the case may be.*)

This delaration must be made before the head of the municipality, and filed among the records of the municipality by the Clerk.

No one can be allowed to inspect ballot papers except by order of a Court or Judge.

The proceedings as to re-count of votes, and contested elections requiring always the aid of a solicitor, it would be useless to fill these pages with a long recital of them.

The Treasurer pays to the Clerk the expenses of the election, and the Clerk distributes them to the several persons entitled.

CHAPTER IV.

MEETINGS OF COUNCILS—VACANCIES IN COUNCILS.

The members of every Municipal Council (except County Councils) hold their first meeting at 11 o'clock a.m. on the third Monday in January " or on some day thereafter."

The members of County Councils hold their first meetings on the fourth Tuesday in January, at two o'clock p.m., "or on some day thereafter."

With regard to the " some day thereafter" above mentioned, it is necessary that the members should all be notified, in case of the meeting not being held on the regular day appointed by statute, but some day afterwards.

No business can be proceeded with at the first meeting of the Council until the declarations of office and qualification have been taken by the members.

DECLARATION OF OFFICE.

The following form of declaration of office is common to all Councillors and officers, excepting auditors. Every Returning Officer, Deputy-Returning Officer, Poll Clerk, member of a Council, Mayor, Clerk, Assessor, Collector, Constable, and other officers appointed by a Council must make this declaration :

I, *A. B.*, do solemnly promise and declare that I will

truly, faithfully and impartially, to the best of my knowledge and ability, execute the office of (*inserting the name of the office*), to which I have been elected (*or appointed*) in this Township (*or as the case may be*), and that I have not received, and will not receive, any payment or reward, or promise of such, for the exercise of any partiality or malversation or other undue execution of the said office, and that I have not by myself or partner, either directly or indirectly, any interest in any contract with or on behalf of the said Corporation.

DECLARATIONS OF QUALIFICATION.

The declaration of qualification is in the following form:—

I, *A.B.*, do solemnly declare that I am a natural born (*or naturalized*) subject of Her Majesty; and have and had to my own use and benefit, in my own right (*or have and had in right of my wife, as the case may be*); as proprietor (*or tenant, as the case may be*), at the time of my election (*or appointment, as the case may require*), to the office of   hereinafter referred to, such an estate as does qualify me to act in the office of (*naming the office*) for (*naming the place for which such person has been elected or appointed*), and that such estate is (*the nature of the estate to be specified, as* an equitable estate of leasehold, *or otherwise as the case may require, and if land, the same to be designated by its local description, rents or otherwise*), and that such estate at the time of my election (*or appointment, as the case may require*) was of the value of at least (*specifying the value*) over and above all charges, liens and incumbrances affecting the same.

But in regard to Township Councillors who qualify as mentioned in the slip attached to page 34, the following is the form to be used:

I, *A.B.*, do solemnly declare that I am a natural born (*or naturalized*) subject of Her Majesty; and have and had to my own use and benefit, in my own right (*or have and had in right of my wife, as the case may be*) as proprietor at the time of my election to the office of   hereinafter referred to, such an estate as does qualify me to act in the office of (*naming the office*) for (*naming the place for which such person has been elected*), and that such estate is (*the nature of the estate to be specified and the land to be designated by its local description*), and that such estate at the time of my election was in my actual occupation, and was actually rated in the then last revised assessment roll of this Township (*naming it*) at an amount not less than $4000.

These declarations may be made before a Court, Judge, Police Magistrate, Justice of the Peace or Clerk. They should be filed with the Clerk.

Besides these declarations, Reeves and Deputy-Reeves must file the certificates of which forms are given on page 31. These are filed with the County Clerk.

A person elected to office who is qualified, must accept the office and make the necessary declarations. In the event of his failure to do so within twenty days from knowing of his election he can be fined at the lowest $8, or at the most $80, on summary conviction before two or more Justices of the Peace.

The members of the County Council elect a Warden at their first meeting, which takes place at the County Hall, if there is one, otherwise at the County Court House. There must be a quorum of the council. The clerk is the presiding officer at the meeting; if there is no clerk, the members select one of themselves to preside, who will have a vote as a member. In the case of an equality of votes on the election of Warden, the Reeve (or in his absence the Deputy-Reeve) of the municipality which has the largest number of names on its last revised assessment roll as ratepayers, has a second, or casting vote.

The meetings of councils other than the first meeting, are held at such place either within or without the municipality, as the council appoints either by resolution on adjourning or by a by-law. They may be held either within or without the municipality.

A county or township council may, besides holding its meetings, keep its offices, transact its business, and the business of its officers in any city, town or village which is situated in the county or township. It may also hold real estate therein for such purposes.

County or township councils may by by-law remunerate the members for attending council or committee meetings. The payment must not be more than $3 a day, and 5 cents per mile, each way, for mileage.

A county, city, town or village council may remunerate its head by an "annual sum." This sum is in the discretion of the council.

Conduct of Business.

Ordinary council meetings must be open, and no person is to be excluded except for improper conduct. Special meetings may be closed if the council passes a resolution to the effect that the public interest requires this to be the case.

A majority constitutes a quorum. Where there are only five members altogether constituting a Council, there must be the concurrent votes of three to carry any resolution or other measure.

The head of every council shall preside at meetings. He may summon special meetings. If a majority of members request it in writing, it is his duty to summon special meetings.

If the head of a council refuse to put a motion, the course for the council to adopt is to vote him out of the chair. Or they may vote on the motion without it being put from the chair.

In the case of the death or absence of the head of a town council, the Reeve presides. In the case of the death or absence of the Mayor and Reeve, then the Deputy-Reeve shall preside. In the case of the death or absence of the head of a village or township council the Deputy-Reeve presides, and may at any time summon a special meeting. If there be more than one Deputy-Reeve, the council shall determine which to preside.

In all councils, where none of the superior officers are present, then the council elects the presiding officer from among themselves. There must be fifteen minutes' grace from the time appointed for meeting, to allow the head of the council to attend.

If during a session of council, the officer who ought to preside enters while another is in the chair, it is a moot question under the statute as to whether the sitting chairman's authority continues for the whole meeting. The proper course, according to high authority, and the usage of parliamentary and deliberative bodies, is for the superior officer to take the presiding place.

The head of the council, or the presiding officer or chairman, may vote with the other members on *all* questions, and any question on which there is an equality of votes shall be deemed to be negatived.

Every council may adjourn its meetings from time

to time.

These rules are statutory. The writer suggests the following additional rules of order adapted from those in use by several municipal councils, as rules of order.

RULES OF ORDER.

So soon after the hour of meeting as there shall be a quorum present the Mayor shall take the chair and call the members present to order.

If the Mayor is not in attendance, the Reeve, or in his absence, the senior Deputy-Reeve present shall call the meeting to order and preside until the arrival of the Mayor or Reeve.

In the absence of the Mayor, Reeve and Deputy-Reeves, one of the councillors present shall be chosen to preside, and shall take the chair and preside during the absence of the Mayor, Reeve and Deputy-Reeves, and at the meeting only at which he has been so chosen.

Immediately after the Mayor or other presiding officer has taken his seat, the minutes of the preceding meeting shall be read by the clerk in order that any mistake therein may be corrected by the Council.

The Mayor or other presiding officer shall preserve order and decorum and decide questions of order subject to an appeal to the Council.

When the Mayor or other presiding officer is called on to decide a point of order or practice he shall state the rule applicable, without argument or comment.

If the Mayor or other presiding officer desires to leave the chair for the purpose of taking part in the debate or otherwise, he shall call a member of the council to fill his place until he resumes the chair.

Every member, previous to his speaking, shall rise from his seat, and shall address himself to the Mayor or other presiding officer.

When two or more members rise at once, the Mayor or other presiding officer shall name the member who first rose in his place, but a motion may be made that any member who has risen "be now heard," or "do now speak."

Every member who shall be present when a question is put, shall vote thereon, unless the Council shall excuse him, or unless he be personally interested in the question, in which case he shall not vote.

A member called to order shall sit down, unless permitted to explain, and the Council, if appealed to, shall decide on the case, but without debate; if there be no appeal, the decision of the Mayor or other presiding officer shall be submitted to.

No member shall speak disrespectfully of the authorities of the country, or use offensive words against the Council or any member thereof, or speak beside the question in debate, or reflect upon any vote of the Council, except for the purpose of moving that such vote be rescinded.

Any member may require the question or motion under discussion to be read at any time during the debate, but not so as to interrupt a member while speaking.

No member shall speak more than once on the same question without leave of the Council, except in explanation of a material part of his speech which may have been misconceived, but then he is not to introduce new matter. A reply is allowed to a member who has made a substantive motion to the Council, but not to any member who has moved an order of the day, an amendment, the previous question, or an instruction to a committee; and no member shall without leave of the Council speak to the same question or in reply, for longer than a quarter of an hour.

Upon a division of the Council, the names of those who vote for, and those who vote against the question, shall be entered upon the minutes, not only in the cases required by law, but when a member shall call for the ayes and nays.

Questions may be put to the Mayor or other presiding officer, or through him to any member of the Council, relating to any bill, motion or other matter connected with the business of the Council or the affairs of the Town, but no argument or opinion is to be offered, or facts to be stated, except so far as may be necessary to explain the same and in answering any such question a member is not to debate the matter to which the same refers.

No person except members or officers of the Council shall be allowed to come within the Bar during the sittings of the Council, without the permission of the Mayor or other presiding officer.

ORDERS OF THE DAY.

1—Reading of Minutes.
2—Original Communications.
3—Petitions.
4—Referring Petitions and Communications.
5—Reports of Committees and consideration thereof.
6—Unfinished Business.
7—Enquiries.
8—Giving Notice.
9—Introduction of Bills.
10—Consideration of Bills.
11—Motions.

The business shall in all cases be taken up in the order in which it stands in the "Orders of the Day," unless otherwise determined upon by a vote of two-thirds of the members present, and without debate thereon.

All motions shall be in writing and seconded before being debated or put from the chair. When a motion is seconded, it shall be read by the Mayor or other presiding officer before debate.

After a motion is read by the Mayor or other presiding officer, it shall be deemed to be in the possession of the Council, but may be withdrawn at any time before decision at the request of the mover and seconder.

A motion of commitment until it is decided, shall exclude all amendments of the main question.

A motion to adjourn shall always be in order, but no second motion to the same effect shall be made until after some intermediate proceedings shall have been had.

When a question is under debate no motion shall be received unless—to commit it; to amend it; to lay on the table; to postpone it; to adjourn; to move the previous question.

The previous question, until it is decided, shall preclude all amendments of the main question, and shall be put without debate, in the following words: "That this question be now put," and if this motion be resolved in the affirmative, the original question is to be put forthwith without any amendment or debate.

All amendments shall be put in the reverse order in which they are moved, except in filling up blanks, when the longest time and the largest sum shall be put first; and every amendment submitted shall be reduced to writing, and be decided upon or withdrawn before the main question is put to vote.

All motions for the appointment of any member of the Council or of any other person, to any office in the gift of the Council, shall preclude any amendments. Only one amendment shall be allowed to an amendment, and any amendment more than one must be made to the main question.

When the question under consideration contains distinct propositions. upon the request of any member, the vote upon each proposition shall be taken separately.

After any question is finally put by the Mayor or other presiding officer, no member shall speak to the question, nor shall any other motion be made until after the result is declared; and the decision of the Mayor or other presiding officer, as to whether the question has been finally put, shall be conclusive.

Whenever the Mayor or other presiding officer is of opinion that a motion offered to the Council is contrary to the rules and privileges of the Council, he shall apprize the members thereof immediately before putting the question thereon, and quote the rule or authority applicable to the case without argument or comment.

No standing rule or order of the Council shall be suspended except by a vote of two-thirds of the members present.

VACANCIES IN COUNCIL.

If, after the election of any member of a Council, he is convicted of a felony or infamous crime, or becomes insolvent

or applies for relief as an indigent debtor,
or remains in close custody,
or assigns his property for the use of his creditors,
or absents himself from the meetings of the Council for three months without being authorized so to do by a resolution of the Council entered on its minutes, his seat in the Council shall thereby become vacant, and the Council shall declare his seat vacant and order a new election.

Any Mayor or other member may with the consent of the majority of the members present to be entered on the minutes of the Council, resign his seat in the Council.

A county warden may resign his office either by verbal intimation to the Council while in session, or by letter to the county clerk if not in session.

In such case, as well as in the case of vacancies by death or otherwise, the clerk shall notify all the members. If a majority of them require it, the clerk shall call a special meeting to fill the vacancy.

New elections to fill vacancies from any cause are held by warrant of the head of the Council directed to the returning officers and deputy returning officers. These must be those who held the last election, or some other person, duly appointed. See page 46 and following pages as to appointment of Returning Officers.

In the case of the head of the Council being absent or his office being vacant, then the clerk acts in his stead. In the case of the clerk also being absent, or his office being vacant, then one of the members of the council can issue the warrant.

The head of the Council of the previous year, or a

Councillor of the previous year issues the warrants when the vacancy occurs previous to the organization of the new Council.

As long as there is a quorum of the full number of a regular Council, any such vacancy or vacancies does not interfere with the organization of a new Council.

It may happen that for some reason or other, independent of riot or other emergency (see page 61) that the electors neglect to elect the Council, or the requisite number of members.

To meet such an event the following provisions are made:—The new members, if they equal or exceed half of the Council when complete, or a majority of such new members, or if a half of such members are not elected, then the members of the preceding year or a majority of them, shall appoint as many qualified persons as will constitute or complete the number of members requisite. The person so appointed shall accept office and make the necessary declarations under the same penalty, in the case of refusal or neglect, as if elected.

CHAPTER V.

MUNICIPAL OFFICERS.

The Head of the Corporation.

In every county the head of the corporation is the Warden, in every city and town, the Mayor, and in every township and village, the Reeve.

The head of the Council is the chief executive officer ; it is his duty, according to the statute—1. To be vigilant and active at all times in causing the law for the government of the municipality to be duly executed and put into force. 2. To inspect the conduct of all subordinate officers. 3. As far as may be in his power to cause all negligence, carelessness and positive violation of duty, to be duly prosecuted and punished. 4. To communicate from time to time to the Council all such information, and recommend such measures within the powers of the Council as may tend to the improvement of the finances, health, security, cleanliness and ornament of the municipality.

The head of Council and the Reeve of every town, township and incorporated village are *ex-officio* Justices of the Peace for the whole county or union of counties in which their respective municipalities lie. Aldermen in cities are Justices of the Peace for such cities.

The Clerk.

It is the duty of every Council to appoint a Clerk.

The duties of the Clerk, according to the statute, are :

1. To truly record, in a book, without note or comment, all resolutions, decisions and other proceedings of the Council.

2. To record, if required by any member present, the name and vote of every member voting.

3. To keep the books, records and accounts of the Council.

4. To preserve and file all accounts acted upon by the Council.

5. To keep in his office or place appointed by by-law of the Council the original or certified copies of all by-laws, and of all minutes and proceedings of the Council.

The Clerk has other duties which are mentioned in other parts of this work.

The Council may make provision for the absence or illness of the Clerk, by either themselves appointing a substitute, or giving him power to appoint one under his hand and seal.

Any inhabitant of the municipality has a right to inspect the records, books, documents, etc., of the corporation on proper occasions, and this right may be enforced by the courts. Any person is entitled to get from the clerk copies of them to be made by the clerk on payment for such copies at the rate of 10 cents for every 100 words, or at any lower rate that the Council appoints. If asked by an elector or other interested person for any certified copy of a by-law, order or resolution, he must give such certificate. The fees, it would seem, though this is not clear, would belong to the municipality, but the

Council may allow them to him.

Returns to be made by Clerks.—The clerk of every city, town and incorporated village and township must on or before the 1st of December in each year, under a penalty of $20, transmit to the Treasurer of Ontario a true return of the *number* of resident ratepayers appearing on the last revised assessment roll of the municipality. This return must be accompanied by an affidavit sworn to before a Justice of the Peace, in the following form:

I, A. B., Clerk of the Municipality of the City, Town, Township or Village (*as the case may be*), of   make oath and say, that the (above, within written, or annexed, *as the case may be*) return, contains a true statement of the number of resident ratepayers appearing on the assessment roll of the said City (Town, Township *or* Village) for the year one thousand eight hundred and

        (Signed) A. B.

Sworn before me, &c.

The clerk of every township, village and town* must under a penalty of $20, within one week after the 1st March in each year, make a return to the county clerk of the following particulars:—

Heads of columns to be varied according to the form of the assessment roll required by law.

1. Number of persons assesssed.
2. Number of acres assessed.
3. Total actual value of real property.
4. Total of taxable incomes.
5. Total value of personal property.
6. Total amount of assessed value of real and personal property.
7. Total amount of taxes imposed by by-laws of the Municipality.
8. Total amount of taxes imposed by by-laws of the County Council.
9. Total amount of taxes imposed by by-laws of any Pro-

---

*As to towns separated from county see page 78.

visional County Council.
10. Total amount of taxes as aforesaid.
11. Total amount of income collected or to be collected from assessed taxes for the use of the Municipality.
12. Total amount of income from Licenses.
13. Total amount of income from Public Works.
14. Total amount of income from shares in incorporated Companies.
15. Total amount from all other sources.
16. Total amount of income from all sources.
17. Total expenditure on account of roads and bridges.
18. Total expenditure on account of other public works and property.
19. Total expenditure on account of stock held in any incorporated Company.
20. Total expenditure on account of Schools and Education, exclusive of School Trustees' Rates.
21. Total expenditure on account of the support of the poor, or charitable purposes.
22. Total expenditure on account of debentures and interest thereon.
23. Total gross expenditure on account of Administration of Justice in all its branches.
24. Amount received from Government on account of Administration of Justice.
25. Total net expenditure on account of Administration of Justice.
26. Total expenditure on account of salaries, and the expenses of Municipal Government.
27. Total number of sheep worried by dogs, and the amount paid therefor by the Municipality.
28. Total expenditure on all other accounts.
29. Total expenditure of all kinds.
30. Total amount of liabilities secured by debentures.
31. Total amount of liabilities unsecured.
32. Total liabilities of all kinds.
33. Total value of real property belonging to the Municipality.
34. Total value of stock in incorporated Companies owned by Municipality.

35. Total amount of debts due to Municipality.
36. Total amount of arrears of taxes.
37. Balance in hands of Treasurer.
38. All other property owned by Municipality.
39. Total assets.

The clerk of every county must before the 1st of April in each year, prepare and transmit to the Provincial Secretary a statement of the aforesaid particulars respecting all the municipalities within his county, entering each municipality in a separate line, with the particulars opposite, each in a separate column, together with the sum total of all the columns for the whole county. He must also make at the same time a return of the same particulars of his own county as a separate municipality, and of the following particulars:

1. Number of Public School Inspectors.
2. Amount paid to School Inspectors.
3. Total amount paid to Sheriffs.
4. Total amount paid to County Crown Attorney.
5. Total amount paid to Clerk of the Peace.
6. Total amount paid for constable and police service.

Every clerk of a city or town separated from the county must make a return to the Provincial Treasurer similar to the one required from clerks or other municipalities to the county clerk.

If default is made in making any of these returns, the County Treasurer or Provincial Secretary, as the case may be, is to retain in his hands any moneys payable to a municipality whose clerk has made default.

The Treasurer.

Every municipality must have a Treasurer. He may be paid by salary or by a per centage. Every Treasurer before entering upon his duties must give such security as the Council directs for the faithful performance of his duties, and especially for duly accounting for and paying all moneys which may come into his hands.

It is the duty of every Council in each year to enquire into the sufficiency of the security of the Treasurer.*

See page 29 as to sureties of a Treasurer in the case of change of a corporation.

The Treasurer shall receive and safely keep all corporation moneys; he shall pay out the same "to such persons and in such manner as the laws of the Province and the lawful by-laws or resolutions of the Council of the municipal corporation whose officer he is, directs."

No member of the Council is to receive from the Treasurer any money for work performed or to be performed. This is to guard against a member's private interest conflicting with his public duty.

If a by-law or resolution is on its face valid, it is sufficient authority if a Treasurer pays money under it. But if a Council appropriates money contrary to statute, the Treasurer is not protected by following this wrongful disposition.

---

*The late Chief Justice Harrison, in his Municipal Manual, remarked that "This is a most important duty, but it is believed, the most neglected of all duties imposed on Councils. It may be that if the municipality loses the benefit of their security by reason of a neglect to perform this duty on the part of the members of the Council, *the latter can be made liable to make good the loss.*" Some defalcations of Treasurers, and the worthless sureties which were found, that the public have witnessed since the words of the Chief Justice were written, emphasize the force of them.

Every Treasurer must make half yearly a statement of assets to be submitted to the Council. See also pages 44 and 45 as to statement of tax defaulters.

When a Treasurer is dismissed from office, or absconds, his successor may draw out any money belonging to the municipality.

ASSESSORS AND COLLECTORS.

Assessors and Collectors are required in every city, town, township and incorporated village. The same person may be appointed Assessor or Collector for more wards than one.

In cities, an Assessment Commissioner may be appointed. He, with the Mayor, appoints such Assessors and Valuators as may be necessary; the Commissioner, Assessors and Valuators constitute a Board of Assessors, which Board has the power of Assessors. The object of forming such a Board is to secure uniformity of Assessment, so that a proper average in all the wards may be reached.

The Council have power by by-law to impose an additional percentage on default of payment of taxes by a day named, which percentage is to be added to the unpaid tax or assessment.

Commissioners, Assessors or Collectors need not be appointed annually; they hold office during the pleasure of the Council.

All notices usually required to be given to the clerk in regard to assessment must, where in cities there is a Commissioner, be given to him.

Where there is a by-law passed, requiring taxes to be paid on or before the 14th December, the Collector must on the 15th December upon oath return the list of tax defaulters to the Treasurer.

AUDITORS.

There are two auditors required to be appointed each year, one by the head of the Council, and the other by the Council itself.

Auditors must not be persons who have any contract or employment, either themselves or in conjunction with any one else, with the corporation. A clerk or Treasurer can not be an auditor. An auditor of a preceding year can be re-appointed; formerly this could not be done.

The auditors' duties are to "examine and report upon all accounts affecting the corporation or relating to any matter under its control or within its jurisdiction." They deal with the previous year ending on 31st December. They are required also to do the following things :—1. Prepare an abstract of the receipts, expenditures, assets and liabilities of the corporation. 2. Prepare a detailed statement of the said particulars in such form as the Council directs. 3. Report in duplicate on all accounts audited by them. 4. Make a special report of any expenditure made contrary to law. 5. File the reports in the office of the clerk within one month after *appointment.*

Any inhabitant or ratepayer has the right to inspect one of the duplicate reports and make a copy or extract at his own expense either by himself or agent.

The clerk must publish the auditors' abstract and report. The detailed statement is to be published in such form as the Council directs. *Copies* of abstracts and statements of minor municipalities in a county must be sent by the clerks to the county clerk, to be kept by him as records.

The Council, upon the report of the auditors, finally audits and allows the accounts of the Treasurer and Collectors and all accounts chargeable to the corporation.

City and town Councils may have an additional audit "daily or otherwise," and appoint an auditor for this purpose. Other Councils may appoint auditors to audit monthly or quarterly. But the appointment of a regular annual auditor is compulsory on all municipalities. The city of Toronto audit is required to be made monthly instead of yearly.

VALUATORS.

For the duty of valuators see afterwards in the chapter on assessment.

POWER TO ADMINISTER OATHS, ETC.

There are certain oaths, affirmations and declarations which may be administered by certain Councillors and others. The persons to whom this power is limited are, "the head of any Council, any Alderman, Reeve or Deputy-Reeve, any Justice of the Peace and Clerk of a municipality."

The oaths, etc., so administered, must relate to the business of the place in which the person administering it holds office.

Where the statute particularly directs, as it does in certain matters, that a certain functionary or official shall administer the oath, then the above mentioned persons have no power to administer it.

The head of every Council, or in his absence the chairman, may administer an oath or affirmation to any person concerning any accounts or other matters submitted to the Council.

Sometimes an oath or affirmation is required. In other cases only a declaration. An oath is where a person swears by calling on the Almighty to witness what he says, either by kissing the Testament or uplifting the hand. An affirmation is where a person affirms without oath; certain persons, according to the necessities of their religious beliefs, are permitted to affirm instead of to swear. People ordinarily, in this country, have no objection to taking the oath, and in such case, they must swear instead of affirming; affirmations are the exception. Declarations are statements taken before some official duly authorized to do so, as for instance, declarations of office, etc., for which see pages 64 and 65.

SALARIES OF OFFICERS.

To entitle any officer to a salary or compensation, it must be expressly given to him either by statute, by-law, resolution or contract.

The Councillors cannot remunerate themselves except as mentioned on page 66.

Where the statute does not fix the salary an officer is entitled to, the Council must provide for the same by a by-law.

No Council is permitted to let out any office by tender so that the lowest bidder is to receive the appointment. This method was found to be such an abuse that the Legislature stepped in and put a special prohibition upon this course being adopted.

A municipal corporation may indemnify an officer against risk of loss, in a matter in which the corporation is interested.

An official holds office until the corporation removes him from office. He is required to perform all duties that statutes may appoint from time to time, or that the Council itself may impose.

Though the appointment of an official may require a seal, yet if he has served the corporation with its consent, he can recover for past services.

Officers who, through old age, have while in service become incapable of efficiently discharging their duties, may receive a gratuity not exceeding the last three years of their salary or remuneration.

It is required in granting of a gratuity like this, that the officer must have been in the service of the municipality for at least twenty years.

Guarantee companies may be accepted as sureties for officials.

CHAPTER VI.

GENERAL POWER OF ALL MUNICIPALITIES.

The powers of municipal corporations are necessarily restricted. Some have more, some less power in certain matters. In still other matters, certain municipal corporations have powers which others do not possess whatever. This is necessary, according to the different circumstances respectively, of town, and country, of the aggregate County Council, and the smaller township body, of the village and the city. Still, there are certain powers and jurisdiction which it is necessary that all municipal councils should possess. In this chapter it is proposed to deal with these *general* powers.

The powers of corporations are restricted to such as are given them by statute. Beyond what the statute gives them, they have none.

The jurisdiction of every Council extends only to the municipality which the Council represents, except in rare instances, where authority is expressly given, as, for instance, in the case of counties having jurisdiction over an adjoining unorganized district.

The general rule is, that a Council must act by by-law. In fact, this general rule is so imperative, that the statute says that "the powers of the council shall be exercised by by-law *when not otherwise authorized or provided for.*" It must, then, be observed that when a resolution or other method acting is not specially mentioned in the statute a by-law is absolutely necessary. As said in Harrison's Municipal Manual,—"whenever a Municipal Council is in doubt whether it can, or can not, do a particular thing by order or resolution, it would be much safer and wiser, owing to the doubt, to use the by-law."

Every Council may make regulations not specifically provided for by the Municipal Act and not contrary to law, for governing the proceedings of the Council, the conduct of the members, the appointing or calling of special meetings, and generally such other regulations as the good of the inhabitants of the municipality requires.

It will be observed that the by laws must not be inconsistent with the Municipal Act, and must not contravene the law of the land. For instance, a Council has no power to alter any of the rules laid down by statute as to elections, and it it passes a by-law for an illegal purpose, the by-law is invalid.

The right to repeal, altar or amend by-laws is of necessity granted to Councils, but there are certain cases where this right is restricted, as mentioned elsewhere: for instance, where debentures are issued under a by-law. such by-law can not be repealed.

The granting of monopolies is prohibited. Likewise the imposition of a special tax on any person exercising a trade or calling. As to licensing a particular trade or calling this subject is treated subsequently. A council may direct a fee not exceeding $1.00 to be paid to the proper officer "for a certificate of compliance" with any regulations in regard to such trade or calling.

A Council may grant exclusive privileges in any ferry which may be vested in the Corporation, but not in any ferry between this Province and another country or province.

By-Laws.

How Authenticated.—By-laws must be,—1. Under the seal of the corporation. 2. Signed by the head of the corporation *or* by the person presiding at the meeting at which the by-law passed,* and 3. Signed by the Clerk. If a by-law is not sealed it is invalid. It would be a safe rule to insist on the seal being applied in open Council.

Where by-laws require the assent of the Lieutenant-Governor, a solemn declaration is required to be made by the head of the Council *and* by the Treasurer and Clerk proving the facts required to be recited in the by-law. In the case of the death or absence of any such municipal officer, then any member of the Council may make the declaration. The Lieutenant-Governor may also require the declarations of others, or other evidence.

Objection by Ratepayers.—When by-laws require the application of ratepayers before they are passed by the Council, then any person rated on the assessment roll is entitled to be heard before the Council in opposition to the by-law; and this either by himself or by his counsel or attorney. He must petition the Council, but after doing so, it is a matter of right that he should be heard.

He may urge the following objections:—

1. That the necessary notice of the application

---

*See page 67 as to another member taking the place of the head of the Council by presiding.

for the by-law was not given.

2. That any of the signatures to the application are not genuine.

3. That some of the signatures were obtained on incorrect statements.

4. That the proposed by-law is contrary to the wishes of the persons whose signatures were so obtained.

5. That the remaining signatures do not amount to the number nor represent the amount of property necessary to the passage of the by-law.

If the Council is satisfied upon the evidence that application for the by-law does not fulfil the requirements just enumerated, the Council should not pass the by-law.

Voting on by-laws by electors.—Whenever the consent of the electors is required to the passing of a by-law, the following are the requisite proceedings:

The Council shall by the by-law fix the day and hour for taking the votes of the electors, and such places in the municipality as they shall in their discretion deem best for the purpose; where the votes are to be taken in more than one place, they shall name the deputy-returning officers. The day fixed for taking the votes shall not be less than three, nor more than five weeks after the first publication.*

A copy must be published in some public newspaper, either of the municipality or county town, or of an adjoining local municipality, as the Council

---

*It has been held that the by-law need not be signed and sealed before publication. The by-law should be read before publication and sanctioned by the Council, but the final reading or passing should not be until after the publication.

may designate by resolution. The publication must be once a week for three successive weeks. A copy must be put up at four or more of the most public places of the municipality.

A notice must be appended to every copy published or posted. This notice is to be signed by the clerk of the Council. The following may be taken as a form.

TAKE NOTICE.—That the above is a true copy of a proposed By-Law, which will be taken into consideration by the Municipal Council of the   , after one month after the first publication thereof in the   , being the newspaper fixed upon by resolution of the said Council, for the publication of this By-Law, and notice, the date of which first publication is   day, the   day of   , in the year of our Lord one thousand eight hundred and eighty   , and that the votes of the duly qualified electors in that behalf will be taken on   day, the   ,   day of   , in the year of our Lord one thousand eight hundred and eighty   , between the hours of nine o'clock in the forenoon, and five o'clock in the afternoon, at the places mentioned in and fixed by the   paragraph of the said above copy of the said proposed By-Law

          A. B.,
           Clerk.

Dated   , 188

The clerk must see to the printing of sufficient ballot papers.

The Council must, *by the by law*, fix a time when and place where the clerk shall sum up the number of votes for and against the by-law, also a time and place for the appointment of persons to attend at the various polling places and at the final summing up of votes respectively on behalf of the persons interested in and promoting or opposing the passage of the by-law respectively.

There are to be two persons appointed by the head of the municipality in a writing signed by him to attend on each summing up of votes. In the same way one on each side is to be appointed to attend at each polling place. Each agent must produce his written appointment to the returning officers.

Each of such persons so appointed is to make a declaration as follows:

> I, the undersigned A. B., do solemnly declare that I am a ratepayer of the Township (*or as the case may be*) of (*The Municipality the Council of which proposes the by-law*), and that I am desirous of promoting (*or opposing, as the case may be*) the passing of the by-law to (*here insert the object of the by-law*), submitted to the Council of said Township (*or as the case may be*).
>
>   (*Signature*)   A. B.
>
> Made and declared before me this
>   day of   , A. D. .
>   C. D.
>   Head of Municipality.

In the absence of any such agent, another person on the same side may take his place on filing a declaration similar to the above, before the clerk or the deputy-returning officer.

The method of polling needs no particular mention, as it is similar to that of ordinary elections, except that attention is necessary to the following special provisions:

Qualification of electors.—Beyond the ordinary qualification, the suffrage is limited to freehold ratepayers either in their own right or the right of their wives. Only such leaseholders are allowed to vote who are resident in the municipality for one month next before the vote, and who are, or whose wives are, leaseholders under a lease extending "for the period of time within which the debt to be contracted or the money to be raised by such by-law is made payable, in which lease the lessee has covenanted to pay all municipal taxes in respect to the property leased."

The two special requirements of the leaseholder voting are these, the time as just quoted over which the lease must extend, and the taxes being required to be paid by the lessee, and not the landlord.

As regards a by-law respecting local improvements, it matters not how long the lease may be, to entitle the leaseholder to vote, but he must pay the taxes.

Unmarried women and widows may vote who possess the property and other qualifications which would, if they were male ratepayers, entitle them to vote.

The following is the form of a freeholder's oath or affirmation:

You swear that you are of the full age of 21 years, and a natural born (or naturalized) subject of Her Majesty.

That you are a freeholder in your own right (or in the right of your wife, *as the case may require*), within the Municipality for which this vote is taken;

That you have not voted before on the by-law in this Township (*or* Ward, *as the case may be*);

That you are, according to law, entitled to vote on the said by-law:

That you have not directly or indirectly received any reward or gift, nor do you expect to receive any, for the vote which you tender;

That you are the person named, or purporting to be named, in the voters' list of the electors;

That you have not received anything, either directly or indirectly, either to induce you to vote on this by-law, or for loss of time, travelling expenses, hire of team or any other service connected therewith;

And that you have not directly or indirectly paid or promised anything to any person, either to induce him to vote or refrain from voting ;

(*In case of a new Municipality in which there has not been any assessment roll, then instead of referring to being named in the voters' list, the person offering to vote may be required to name in the oath the property in respect of which he claims to vote*).

The following is the form of a leaseholder's oath or affirmation :

You swear that you are of the full age of 21 years, and a natural born (or naturalized) subject of Her Majesty ;

That you have been a resident within the Municipality for which this vote is taken for one month next before the vote;

That you are (*or* your wife is), a leaseholder within this Municipality, and the lease extends for the period of time within which the debt to be contracted or the money to be raised by the by-law now submitted to the ratepayers is made payable, and that you have (*or* that the lessee in said lease has) covenanted in such lease to pay all municipal taxes ;

That you have not before voted on the by-law in this Township (*or* Ward, *as the case may be*) ;

That you are, according to law, entitled to vote on the said by-law;

That you have not directly or indirectly received any reward or gift, nor do you expect to receive any, for the vote which you tender ;

That you are the person named, or purporting to be named, in the voters' list;

That you have not received anything, nor has anything been promised to you directly or indirectly, either to induce you to vote on this by-law, or for loss of time, travelling expenses, hire of team, or any other service connected therewith ;

And that you have not directly or indirectly paid or promised anything to any person, either to induce him to vote or refrain from voting ;

(In case of a new Municipality in which there has not been any assessment roll, then instead of swearing to residence for one month next before the vote, and instead of referring to being named in the voters' list, the person offering to vote may be required to name in the oath the property in respect of which he claims to vote, and that he is a resident of such Municipality.)

The following is the form of a leaseholder's oath or affirmation who votes on a by-law respecting local improvements.

You swear that you are of the full age of 21 years, and a natural born (*or* naturalized) subject of Her Majesty ;

That you have been a resident within the Municipality for which this vote is taken for one month next before the vote ;

That you are (*or* your wife is) a leaseholder within this Municipality, and that you have (*or* the lessee in said lease has) covenanted in such lease to pay all Municipal taxes ;

That you have not before voted on the by-law in this Township (*or* Ward, *as the case may be*) ;

That you are, according to law, entitled to vote on the said by-law ;

That you have not directly or indirectly received any reward or gift, nor do you expect to receive any, for the vote which you tender ;

That you are the person named, or purporting to be named, in the voters' list ;

That you have not received anything, nor has anything been promised to you either directly or indirectly, either to induce you to vote on this by-law, or for loss of time, travelling expenses, hire of team, or for any other service connected therewith ;

And that you have not directly or indirectly paid or promised anything to any person, either to induce him to vote or refrain from voting ;

(In case of a new Municipality in which there has not been any assessment roll, then instead of swearing to residence for one month next before the vote, and of being named in the voters' list, the person offering to vote may be required to name in the

oath the property in respect of which he claims to vote, and that he is a resident of such Municipality.

With regard to unmarried women and widows being required to take an oath or affirmation, there is no special provision in the statute for them. It may be that they would be required to take the oath leaving out the clause which reads "that you are the person named, or purporting to be named, in the voters' list." Or this clause may be left in and have it refer to the list used by the deputy returning officer. In the absence of authority it is hard to venture an opinion as to whether women are or are not required to take an oath. It would seem to be an oversight of the legislature, or perhaps the omission was designedly made in a spirit of gallantry towards the unmarried women and widows.

Returns of voting.—The duties of clerk and deputy returning officers are the same in regard to return of ballots, certificates, declarations, etc., as in ordinary municipal elections, except as to the additional certificate mentioned below.

The remarks made in Chapter III may be read as applying for the most part, where applicable, to voting on by-laws by electors.

Necessary votes to carry certain by-laws.—To render valid a by-law of any municipality for (1) granting a bonus in aid of a railway, or (2) for promoting any manufacture, or (3) for taking stock in any railway company, (4) or for lending money to such company (5) or for guaranteeing the payment of money borrowed by any such company, (6) or for lending money to any other company or person on condition of such company or person establishing or continuing a manufactory in or near such municipality, the assent shall be necessary of *two-fifths* of all ratepayers who are entitled to vote, as well as of a majority of the ratepayers voting on the by-law.

The clerk must, in making his return of the voting, when a majority of the ratepayers are in favor of the by-law, also certify whether or not such majority appears (as shown by the voters' list and assessment roll) to be two-fifths of all the voters who are entitled to vote on the by-law.

An example of the rule requiring two-fifths, may be given as follows:—Suppose that there are 1,000 persons entitled to vote, as shewn by the voters' list and assessment roll. If the poll stands 375 for the by-law, 150 against, then the by-law is lost, because 375 is less than two-fifths of 1,000—viz: 400. Thus every voter absenting himself from the poll practically votes against the by-law.

Passing of the by-law by the Council.—The Council must within six weeks after the by-law being carried by the votes of the electors, pass it finally. But in case there happens to be a petition presented against the by-law, the Council must dispose of the petition before passing the by-law. The time between receiving and disposing of the petition is not to be reckoned as part of the six weeks just spoken of.

CONFIRMATION OF BY-LAWS.

Whenever a by-law is required to be promulgated the following notice is to be published :

NOTICE —The above is a true copy of a by-law passed by the Municipal Council of the   of   on the   day of   A. D. 18   and approved by His Honor, the Lieutenant-Governor in Council, on the   day of

A. D. 18   (*where such approval is required to give effect to such by-law*): And all persons are hereby required to take notice that anyone desirous of applying to have such by-law, or any part thereof, quashed, must make his application for that purpose to the High Court of Justice, Toronto, within three months next after the publication of this notice once a week for three successive weeks, in the newspaper called the   or he will be too late to be heard in that behalf.

This notice is to be published "in such public newspaper published either within the municipality, or in the county town, or in a public newspaper published in an adjoining local municipality *as the Council may designate by resolution.*" The notice must be published at least once a week for three successive weeks.

With regard to quashing by-laws, the assistance of a lawyer being required in proceedings to quash them, it would be superfluous in this handbook to detail them at length.

BY-LAWS CREATING DEBTS.

A Municipal Council may under the formalities required by law.

1. Pass by-laws for contracting debts by borrowing money or otherwise.

2. And for levying rates for payment of such debts on the rateable property of the municipality for any purpose within the jurisdiction of the Council.

By-laws of this kind are under certain imperative restrictions which need to be carefully considered and attended to.

If a by-law of this kind is for any other purpose than the purchase of public works, it must name a day in the financial year, in which it is passed, when the by-law is to take effect.

The debt must not extend for more than 20 years beyond the time when the by-law is to take effect. As to gas or water works it may extend to 30 years. As to purchase of public works see page 99.

There must be a rate to meet the interest, also a sinking fund rate to meet the principal.

With regard to these rates, in calculating the rate for redeeming the principal, the estimated interest to be earned by the corporation is to be taken into account, so that the rate itself and the interest which will accrue upon the rate will meet the principal when due. No such estimated interest is to be estimated at more than five per cent. per annum to be capitalized yearly.

The by-law should provide an annual rate on all the rateable property. The annual rate should be uniform for all the years. The by-law should recite (1,) the amount and object of the debt, (2,) the amount to be raised annually, (3,) the amount of the whole rateable property of the municipality according to the last revised, or revised and equalized assessment roll, and (4,) the amount of the existing debenture debt, and of the principal and interest in arrears.

What has just been said in the last paragraph does not apply to by-laws for works payable by local assessment. They need to provide that the annual rate shall be raised and levied on all the property rateable under the by-law or per foot frontage as the case may be. They should recite 1. Amount and object of debt. 2. Amount to be raised annually. 3. Value of real property rateable. 4. That debt is created on security of special rate, and on that security only.

The principal of a debt may be made payable in annual instalments. In this case the interest will of course be reduced from year to year, and it is an undecided question as to whether the rate must be the same every year. The wording of the statute is "equal, nearly as may be."

By-laws for raising money not for ordinary expenses must receive the assent of the electors. This is when the money is not payable within the same municipal year. Drainage by-laws, which will be specially treated of hereafter, are not within this rule. Counties also may to the extent of $20,000 in any one year raise money by by-law, over and above ordinary expenditure. But there must be a special meeting of the County Council called for the purpose and a copy of the by-law published and a notice provided by statute as follows :

The above is a true copy of a proposed by-law to be taken into consideration by the Municipality of the County (*or* United Counties) of   , at   , in the said County (*or* United Counties), on the   day of   , 18 , at the hour of   o'clock in the   noon, at which time and place the members of the Council are hereby required to attend for the purpose aforesaid.

G. H.,
Clerk.

The by-law and notice must be published weekly in a newspaper in the County, or if there is no such newspaper, then in a newspaper published nearest the county.

Where part only of money has been raised the by-law may be repealed as to residue. In such case the by-law should: 1. Recite the facts on which it is founded. 2. Be appointed to take effect on the 31st December in the year of its passing. 3. Not affect any rate due or penalties incurred before that day. 4. Be first approved by the Lieut.-Governor in Council.

Until the debt contracted by the corporation has been paid, the Council can not repeal, alter, or amend the by-law creating it except as above, and in case such an illegal repealing by-law has been passed, no officer can neglect or refuse to carry into effect the by-law creating the debt.

Purchase of Public Works.—Public roads, harbors, bridges, buildings or other public works belonging either to the Dominion or the Province may be purchased by municipal corporations without the necessary by-law specifying any annual or other rate to be imposed. The rate to be imposed may be such as the Council "may deem expedient" to use the words of the statute, so that the rate is a matter in the discretion of the Council.

Registration of By-Laws.—Where debentures are to run longer than a year, the by-law authorizing them must be registered by the Clerk within two weeks after its passing.

The by-laws are registered in the registry office, of the registration division in which the municipality is situate. In the case of a county where there is more than one registry office, they are registered in the registry office in the county town. The registrar's fee is $2.

It is optional, but not compulsory, to register by-laws relating to local improvements.

The time within which application to quash a by-law must be made is three months from registration.

When a registered by-law is not such a one as must be submitted to the ratepayers, the following notice must be published :

<blockquote>
Notice is hereby given that a by-law was passed by the ———— of ———— of ———— on the ———— day of ———— A.D., 18——, providing for the issue of debentures to the amount of $ ———— for the purpose of ———— and that such by-law was registered in the registry office of ———— the county of ———— on the ———— day of ———— A.D. 18——

Any motion to quash or set aside the same or any part thereof must be made within three months from the date of registration and cannot be made therafter.

Dated the ———— day of ———— 18——

Clerk.
</blockquote>

This notice must be published " in some public newspaper published either within the municipality or in the county town or in a public newspaper in an adjoining local municipality *as the Council may designate by resolution.*" It must be once a week for three successive weeks.

By-Laws Respecting Yearly Rates.

Yearly rates, which are rates for debts falling due within the year, cannot be higher than two cents in the dollar on the actual value. This is besides school rates.

The object of the law in making Councils provide to meet their liabilities within a year, by a rate of the year itself, is to make each year provide for itself, and prevent Councils of one year from burthening future Councils with their debts.

To the limit of two cents in the dollar there are exceptions provided in the cases of municipalities where the aggregate amount required for the "current annual expenses" *and* the interest and the principal of the debts contracted by such municipalities on 29th March, 1873, exceed the aggregate rate of two cents in the dollar.

The explanation of this is, that the limit of two cents in the dollar was first established by a statute passed on 29th March, 1873. The object of the Legislature was to restrain the incurring of debts by municipalities, but in restraining them as to the future, the Legislature thought it necessary not to prevent municipalities from liquidating obligations already incurred. Such municipalities must not contract further debts until they reduce the rate within two cents in the dollar.

There may also be an exception to the restriction when the legislature provides by a special act for a particular purpose that the rate may be exceeded. This is done sometimes in aid of local railway enterprises.

The rate must be levied on the actual *value* of property. Thus a rate of so much per acre is illegal.

The estimates must be made each year, and in regard to them the Council must take into considertion (1) the cost of collection of the rate, and (2) the abatement and losses which may occur in its collection as well as (3) such taxes on the lands of non-residents as may not be collected.

A local municipality has not the power to impose a rate in aid of a County rate.

The rate is levied under authority of a by-law

or by-laws passed for the purpose. A by-law of this kind should recite the amount proposed to be raised, when payable, and the whole amount of the rateable property according to the last revised or equalized assessment rolls.

If the amount collected falls short of the sums required, the Council may direct the deficiency to be made up from any unappropriated fund belonging to the municipality. If there is no unappropriated fund the deficiency may be equally deducted from the estimates, or any part of them.

If the amount collected exceeds the estimates, then the excess belongs to the general fund, except when the excess collected is in a special tax upon a particular locality; in such case the appropriation must be appropriated to the special local object.

The financial year begins 1st January and ends 31st December. Taxes are due from 1st January, unless the Council directs a different time for them to be due.

There is a special provision relating to Debentures issued before 1st January 1867. The necessity of this provision is, that before this date, in cities, towns and villages, yearly and not actual values prevailed, and so the by-laws of these municipalities had to be based upon yearly values. Debentures were issued on the security of such values and rights acquired by the purchasers of them that such values should until the payment of the debentures be maintained. The statute declares in effect that these rights shall be maintained by the levy of a rate on the actual real value, sufficient to produce a sum equal to that leviable or produced on the yearly values of property as established by the assessment of 1866. These rates are to be applied in payment of these debentures, which are to have the same order of priority as they occupied on 1st January 1867.

ANTICIPATORY APPROPRIATIONS.

The Municipal Act enacts as follows:—

371. In case any Council desires to make an anticipatory appropriation for the next ensuing year, in lieu of the special rate for such year in respect of any debt, the Council may do so, by by-law, in the manner and subject to the provisions and restrictions following:—

(1) The Council may carry to the credit of the sinking fund account of the debt, as much as may be necessary for the purpose aforesaid ;

(a) Of any money at the credit of the special rate account of the debt beyond the interest on such debt for the year following that in which the anticipatory appropriation is made ;

(b) And of any money raised for the purpose aforesaid by additional rate or otherwise ;

(c) And of any money derived from any temporary investment of the sinking fund ;

(d) And of any surplus money derived from any corporation work or any share or interest therein ;

(e) And of any unappropriated money in the treasury ;*

---

*A Council should not take moneys already appropriated and apply them to purposes different to those they were originally appropriated for. It has been decided in the Court of Queen's Bench that this can not be done in the case of appropriations to the sinking fund account of the debt.

Such moneys respectively not having been otherwise appropriated.

(2) The by-law making the appropriations shall distinguish the several sources of the amount, and the portions thereof to be respectively applied for the interest and for the sinking fund appropriation of the debt for such next ensuing year.

(3) In case the moneys so retained at the credit of the special rate account, and so appropriated to the sinking fund account from all or any of the sources above mentioned, are sufficient to meet the sinking fund appropriation and interest for the next ensuing year, the Council may then pass a by-law directing that the original rate for such next ensuing year be not levied.

872. The by-law shall not be valid unless it recites:

(*a*) The original amount of the debt, and in brief and general terms, the object for which the debt was created ;

(*b*) The amount, if any, already paid of the debt;

(*c*) The annual amount of the sinking fund appropriation required in respect of such debt;

(*d*) The total amount, then on hand, of the sinking fund appropriations, in respect to the debt, distinguishing the amount thereof in cash in the treasury from the amount temporarily invested ;

(*e*) The amount required to meet the interest of the debt for the year next after the making of such anticipatory appropriation ; and

(*f*) That the Council has retained at the credit of the special rate account of the debt, a sum sufficient to meet the next year's interest (naming the amount of it), and that the Council has carried to the credit of the sinking fund account a sum sufficient to meet the sinking fund appropriation (naming the amount of it) for such year.

(2) No such by-law shall be valid unless approved by the Lieutenant-Governor in Council.

373. After the dissolution of any Municipal Union, the Senior Municipality may make an anticipatory appropriation for the relief of the Junior Municipality, in respect of any debt secured by the by-law, in the same manner as the Senior Municipality might do on its own behalf.

FINANCES.

Every municipal corporation must keep two accounts; one, the special rate account, and the other the sinking fund or instalments account. These directions are imperative, and the readers' attention is specially directed to sections 374 to 384 of the statute, which contain in themselves sufficient directions without any other comment.

A commission of enquiry may be had into the financial affairs of the corporation. This commission would be issued by the Provincial Government at the instance of one-third of the members of the Council, or thirty duly qualified electors of the Municipality.

CHAPTER VII.

ARBITRATIONS.

Appointment of Arbitrators.—Arbitrators on behalf of a corporation should be appointed by by-law and under the corporate seal, and authenticated by the signature of the head, and of the clerk.

The appointment of an arbitrator may be made by the head of the Council, when the Council gives him the power, under a by-law for the purpose to make the appointment.

Each party appoints an arbitrator, and gives notice thereof to the other party.

A third arbitrator is appointed by the two so chosen. This third one, must be appointed within seven days from the time of appointment of the last of the two appointed.

When more than two municipalities have an arbitration and there is an equality of arbitrators, they must appoint another. In default of their doing so, in 21 days, the Lieutenant-Governor, on application of any Municipality, will appoint such arbitrator.

In the case of arbitrations between townships, or between a township and a town or incorporated village the third arbitrator may be appointed by the County Judge.

Between Corporations and Individuals.—There may be arbitration between a corporation and the owner of real property taken or injured by the corporation.

In such case the first appointment is made by the individual, and the corporation must within seven days after notice, appoint a second arbitrator, and give notice. The Council in this kind of arbitration must express "what powers the Council intends to exercise with respect to the property, describing it."

When the initiative is not taken by the individual, the course to be adopted is as follows :—The Council has him served with a copy of the by-law, certified under the hand of the Clerk, and if the person so notified fails within 21 days to name an arbitrator and give notice, then the Council may appoint an arbitrator. The individual then has seven days to appoint one.

When there are several persons and the Council seeks to include them in one arbitration, as having interests in the one property, or in parts of it, then they have 21 days instead of 7, to appoint an arbitrator for themselves jointly.

Failure to Appoint an Arbitrator.—In case of any failure to appoint an arbitrator then the County Judge appoints one for the party or parties failing to appoint. He also appoints the third arbitrator. An arbitrator appointed by him must not be a resident of the municipality.

Time for Making Award.—The arbitrators must make their award within one month from the appointment of the third arbitrator.

Persons Disqualified as Arbitrators.—Councillors or officers of an interested municipality can not be arbitrators.

Oath of Arbitrator.—The following oath* must before the arbitration takes place be taken by each arbitrator before a Justice of the Peace:

"I (A. B.) do swear (*or affirm*) that I will well and truly try the matters referred to me by the parties, and a true and impartial award make in the premises, according to the evidence and my skill and knowledge. So help me God."

This oath must be signed by him.

Time of Meeting, etc.—The arbitrators must meet within twenty days after the appointment of the third arbitrator. Their award must be in writing. If it is respecting drainage work, it must be in triplicate, one copy to be registered in the Registry office. All awards must be filed with the clerks of municipalities interested.

They have discretion as to awarding how costs are to be paid.

Notes of evidence must be taken and filed with the clerk, as well as documentary evidence or a copy thereof. If they proceed on a view by themselves, or use their own knowledge in arriving at a decision, they must put a statement thereof in writing.

Where in regard to property to be entered upon or taken from individuals, the by-law does not authorize the entry on, or taking of the property before the making of the award. And when the by-law has authorized the taking or entry on the property, but the arbitrators find that the authority has not been acted upon, they have the same period.

---

*Though appointed by a particular side, an arbitrator should remember that he is not to act on behalf of that side; he is to act impartially, being placed in a judicial position. He is judge of law and facts.

In cases of this kind no notes of the evidence need be written. In the event of the failure of the corporation to adopt the award, the by-law is considered repealed, and the corporation must pay the costs of the arbitration.

Awards must be signed by all or two of the arbitrators, the decision of the majority being binding.

Awards are subject to revision by the High Court of Justice.

CHAPTER VIII.
POLICE OFFICE, MAGISTRATE, COMMISSIONERS, ETC., IN CITIES AND TOWNS.—COURT HOUSE, GAOLS, ETC.

Police Office.—In every city and town there must be a police office. Where there is a Police Magistrate he attends daily, or as often as necessary. In his absence or in case there is no Police Magistrate then the Mayor attends. Justices of the Peace may act at the request either of the Police Magistrate, or Mayor, where there is no Police Magistrate.

Except in cases of urgent necessity no attendance is required on Sundays, Christmas Day, Good Friday, days appointed for Fast or Thanksgiving or Civic Holidays.

Duties of Clerks.—City and Town Clerks, are Clerks of Police Courts. When paid by fixed salary their fees belong to the Municipality.

Salaries of Police Magistrates.—The salaries of Police Magistrates are fixed by statute as follows:—

In cities,	$1,400 a year.
In towns of 6,000 inhabitants and under	800 "
" between 6,000 and 8,000	1,000 "
" over 8,000	1,200 "

Police Magistrates' salaries are payable by the city or town, half yearly.

No salaried Police Magistrate is appointed for a

town not having more than 5,000 inhabitants, until two-thirds of the members of the Town Council pass a resolution affirming the expediency thereof, and the Council may by such resolution fix the salary.

Any Police Magistrate appointed before the 29th March, 1873, is not affected by the above rules as to any salary he was then entitled to.

POLICE COMMISSIONERS.

Every city must have a Board of Police Commissioners. With towns, it is optional to have such a Board. The Board is fixed by statute as follows:—
The Mayor, the County Judge, and the Police Magistrate.*

A Town having Police Commissioners, may at any time by by-law dissolve the Board.

The Board has powers delegated it, which ordinarily belong to Councils these being the power of licensing livery stables, cabs, etc., in cities and appointment and control of the police force.

With regard to the licensing, etc., of livery stables and cabs, they have also the power to regulate the rates of fare to be taken by the owners or drivers. This would relate to travel within the city. It is the owner, however, and not the driver of a cab who is required to take out a license.

Until the organization of a Board of Police, every Mayor or Police Magistrate may, within his jurisdiction, suspend from office for any period in his dis-

---

*In case the office of County Judge or that of Police Magistrate is vacant, the Council of the City *shall*, and the Council of the town *may* appoint a resident (or two residents as the case may be) of the city or town, to be members of the Board during such vacancy.

cretion, the Chief Constable, or any Constable of the town or city. He may, if he chooses, appoint some other person to the office during such period. In case he considers the suspended officer deserving of dismissal, he shall, immediately after suspending him report the case to the Council; the Council may then dismiss or it may direct him to be restored to his office after the period of his suspension.

During the suspension such officer shall not be entitled to any salary.

While the appointment of Chief of Police or Constables is in the hands of the Commissioners in a City, the Council have the appointment of and must appoint a High Bailiff, but it may provide by by-law that the office of High Bailiff and Chief Constable may be held by the same person.

Court Houses, Gaols, etc.

Court Houses, Gaols, Houses of Correction, and Houses of Industry, are erected by County Councils, and it is their duty to keep them (when erected) in repair, and to provide food, fuel and other supplies necessary for them. As to Gaols, there is a special provision empowering the Inspector of Asylums to report on them, and in the event of the County Council failing to make the necessary repairs required by the Inspector's report, (which is subject to revision by the Lieut.-Governor) they may be compelled to make the repairs at the instance of the Attorney-General or any private prosecutor.

City Councils may erect, preserve, improve and provide for the proper keeping of a Court House, Gaol, House of Correction, and a House of Industry upon land being the property of the municipality, and may pass by-laws for any or all of these purposes.

A Lock-up House is a place where persons are temporarily confined, or committed for a short space of time.*

Lock-up Houses may be established by County Councils and a constable placed in charge, such constable being appointed at the General Sessions of the Peace. His salary is to be paid by the County, or he may be paid by fees.

Lock-up Houses under the jurisdiction of cities, towns, townships and incorporated villages, are where prisoners may be confined in the following cases :—

1. Where they are *sentenced* to imprisonment for not more than ten days, *under a by-law of the Council.*

2. When they are *detained* for examination on the charge of having committed any offence.

3. When they are *detained* for transmission to the Common Gaol or House of Correction.

The local Councils, have the same powers in regard to Lock-up Houses as are possessed by County Councils.

Two or more Municipalities may unite to establish and maintain a Lock-up House.

Two or more municipalities may unite to establish a Lock-up House.

Land may be acquired by any county, city or

---

* Lock up Houses are very often badly kept, there being no institutions which, as a rule, are so neglected as they are. It ought to be remembered that prisoners are human beings, and whether they are innocent or guilty, there ought to be some approach to decency in maintaining these Lock up Houses.

town separated from the county for Industrial Farms, Houses of Industry and Houses of Refuge, and they may be kept up, and the necessary officials appointed and in general governed by the municipality.

Any two or more of contiguous municipalities may unite in having these institutions.

The persons liable to be committed to the House of Correction or to the Industrials Farms are "such description of persons as may by the Council be deemed and by by-law be declared expedient." They may be committed either with or without hard labor. Persons of the following classes are particularly pointed out as fit subjects for confinement in Houses of Industry and Refuge :

"(1). All poor and indigent persons who are incapable of supporting themselves ;

"(2.) All persons without the means of maintaining themselves, and able of body to work, and who refuse or neglect so to do ;

"(3.) All persons leading a lewd, dissolute or vagrant life, and exercising no ordinary calling, or lawful business sufficient to gain o procure an honest living ;

"(4.) And all such as spend their time and property in public houses, to the neglect of any lawful calling ;

"(5.) And idiots."

The object of Houses of Correction as distinguished from Gaols, is to imprison such individuals, who, although not criminals, lead idle, disorderly or vagrant lives. Where there is no House of Correction the county gaol is to be used for this purpose.

The sheriff has the care of the gaol, gaol office,

yard and gaolers' apartments, and the appointment of the gaoler and turnkeys, but every appointment or dismissal of a gaoler is subject to the approval of the Ontario Government. The salaries are by the County Council subject to the revision or requirement of the Provincial Inspector of Prisons.

The County Council has the care of the Court House, and all the offices in connection with it, whether the Court House is connected with the gaol, or forms a separate building. The county council must make all necessary provisions for the accommodation of the Courts of Justice, excepting Division Courts.

There is no city in Ontario separated from a county for Judicial purposes. In the event of such being the case, a city will have a Court House and gaol separate from that of the county.

Cities and towns separated from the county (for municipal purposes) must bear their share of expenses for judicial purposes, and as part of these expenses they must bear the expense of building, repairing and maintaining Court House and gaol, including lighting, heating, furniture, etc.; as well as these expenses for the offices connected with the courts, they must also contribute to the expenses of criminal justice, except constables' fees, and the charges connected with coroner's inquests, and also excepting such other charges as the counties are entitled to be repaid by the Province.

In the event of the city or town and county not being able to agree as to their respective proportion of such expenses, then the dispute is to be settled by arbitration. See preceding chapter.

If, after the lapse of five years after agreement between the corporations as to the proportion of expenses to be borne by them, or after an award by arbitration, as the case may be, either corporation applies to the Ontario Government, and the Government thinks it reasonable that the amount of compensation should be reconsidered, they may by an Order in Council direct the existing arrangement to cease after a time named in the order. There must then be a new agreement or arbitration.

In the erection of a Court House or jaol, a city is to have a voice in the selection of the site. If the city and county fail to agree, then the dispute is to be settled by arbitration.

There is a special provision to the effect that counties are liable only for such furniture as they have ordered or given authority to order. This is to prevent officials from procuring furniture without being authorized.

CHAPTER IX.

INVESTIGATION INTO THE CONDUCT OF OFFICIALS.

Any Council may by passing a resolution request the County Judge to enquire into any of the following matters :—

1. A supposed malfeasance, breach of trust or other misconduct on the part of any member of the Council or officer of the corporation.
2. Or any person having a contract therewith.
3. Any matter connected with the good government of the municipality or the conduct of any part of the public business thereof.

A simple resolution containing a request to the County Judge is all that is required. It then becomes the duty of the Judge to investigate and he has the power to examine witnesses upon oath. After the investigation is concluded he reports to the Council the result of the enquiry and the evidence taken.

Besides the investigation into matters above provided for, the attention of the reader is directed to page 105, where investigation into the finances of a corporation is spoken of.

CHAPTER VIII.
POWERS OF PARTICULAR MUNICIPAL COUNCILS.

In Chapter VI. general powers possessed by *all* municipalities were treated of. It was then said in introducing the subject, that "the powers of municipal corporations are necessarily restricted. Some have more, some less power in certain matters. In still other matters certain municipal corporations have powers which others do not possess whatever." That chapter treated, as has just been said, of general powers which all Councils possess; the present chapter will treat of powers which particular Councils only possess.

In the nature of our complex municipal system, and in the different necessities of town and country municipalities, there are certain powers suitable to one municipality that are not suitable to another. For instance, cities and towns require certain powers which are not necessary to a township and *vice versa*. Then counties need certain powers which subordinate municipalities cannot possess.

Owing to the complicated requirements of the different municipalities it has been necessary in the framing of the Municipal Act to group them into certain divisions according to the powers they possess. These divisions are as follows:—

Div. I.—Of Counties, Townships, Cities, Towns, and Incorporated Villages.

Div. II.—Of Townships, Cities, Towns and Incorporated Villages.

Div. III.—Of Councils of Counties and Cities.

Div. IV.—Of Counties, Cities and Separated Towns.

Div. V.—Of Cities, Towns and Incorporated Villages.

Div. VI.—Of Cities and Towns.

Div. VII.—Of Towns and Incorporated Villages.

Div. VIII.—Of Counties only.

Div. IX.—Of Townships only.

In observing these groups of municipalities, to ascertain the powers possessed by them, it is well to see in each instance,—firstly, what municipalities are mentioned, and secondly, any municipality that is omitted. By following this rule the powers of the various councils will be easily discerned.

In treating of the different powers, the writer finds that to treat of them all at length would expand this hand-book into a large volume. Owing to the limited space the matters that are of most importance will alone be treated of at any length.

DIVISION I.—POWERS OF COUNCILS OF COUNTIES, TOWNSHIPS, CITIES, TOWNS AND INCORPORATED VILLAGES.

Obtaining Property.—A municipal corporation can not acquire land for speculation or profit, except that wet lands as mentioned hereafter may be so acquired by them. The law allows a corporation to obtain such real and personal property as may be required for the use of the corporation, for erecting a hall, and other necessary municipal buildings. These buildings should be erected on land belonging to the corporation.

Appointing Officers.—Besides the other necessary officials, a municipal corporation has the power to appoint the following:—

Pound-keepers,   Road Surveyors,
Fence Viewers,   Road Commissioners,
Overseers of Highways, Valuators,
            Game Inspectors,

and while the general rule is that a Councillor can not be appointed to any office in the gift of the Council, or have any contract with the corporation, still, it is expressly provided that a Councillor may act as commissioner, superintendent or overseer over any road or work of the municipality. And he may be paid by the Council.

Harbors, docks, etc.—A Council may pass by laws to prevent the encumbering, injuring or fouling of harbors, docks, wharves, drains, sewers, shores, bays or rivers. And it may cause obstructions to wharves, etc., to be removed at the expense of the owner or occupant of the property on which these obstructions may be.

A Council may make and maintain wharves, docks, and prevent the filling up of harbors; and erect and maintain the necessary beacons; and rent wharves, elevators, etc., regulate the vessels, etc., arriving in the harbor; and impose and collect such reasonable harbor dues as may serve to keep the harbor in good order, and pay a harbor master.

It may grant aid by way of bonus towards the construction of harbors, etc.

Aiding Agricultural and other Societies.—A Council may grant money or land in aid of the Agricultural and Arts Association of Ontario, or of any duly organized Agricultural or Horticultural Society in Ontario, or of any incorporated Mechanics' Institute within the municipality, or within any adjoining municipality.

Aiding Manufacturing Establishments.—Manufacturing establishments may be aided by corporations by way of bonus. This may be done either by one sum or by annual or other payments. The parties aided may be restricted as to terms, and may be required to give security by mortgage or otherwise.*

In a case where the majority of the members of the Council granting the bonus were also stockholders in the concern to be benefited the court held that the bonus by-law was invalid. See page 36. The assent of the electors is required to a by-law granting a bonus in aid of a manufactory. An elector who is a shareholder in a company applying for a bonus has no right to vote on the by-law.

Aiding Road Companies, etc.—Stock may be taken, money may be lent, or a bonus given to any incorporated company in respect of any road, bridge or harbor within or near the municipality. The assent of the electors is necessary. See the Act relating to Joint Stock Road Companies, Revised Statutes of Ontario, chap. 152.

Indigent persons and Charities.—It is in the discretion of municipalities to aid indigent persons in workhouses, hospitals, insane, deaf and dumb or blind asylums, etc. They may also grant aid to charitable institutions or out-door relief to the resi-

---

*Exemption from taxation may be given for a period not longer than ten years. Such exemption may be given to either a new or an old manufactory.

dent poor.

Census.—A Municipal Council may have a census taken of the inhabitants or of the resident male freeholders and householders.*

Driving on Roads and Bridges.—A Council may regulate the driving and riding of horses and other cattle on highways and bridges, and prevent racing, immoderate or dangerous driving or riding.

In addition to this provision, a general statute enacts that any person who has the superintendence or management of a bridge over 30 ft. in length may put up a notice legibly printed in the following form:

"Any person or persons riding or driving over this bridge at a faster rate than a walk, will on conviction thereof be subject to a fine, as provided by law."

Upon such notice being posted, any person so riding or driving faster than a walk may be fined not less than $1, nor more than $20 and costs. See Rev. Stat. chap. 183.

Drainage.—Drains, sewers and water courses may be opened, made, preserved, improved, repaired, widened, altered, diverted, stopped up, or pulled down by municipal corporations; and land may be entered upon, broken up, taken or used in any way necessary or convenient for these purposes. As to this subject, see the latter part of this chapter under the head, "*Compensation for lands taken.*"

Egress from Buildings.—Owing to many serious casualties to life, which have resulted in times of panic from overcrowded assemblies seeking egress from public buildings, it has been enacted that municipalities may pass by-laws regulating the size and

---

*The Dominion census, under the supervision of the Canadian Government, is taken every ten years.

number of doors in churches, theatres, halls or other public buildings; the street gates leading thereto as well as the size and structure of stairs and stair railings, and the strength of beams, joists and supports are similarly provided for.

Fines and Penalties.—The imposition of fines and penalties may be enacted by Municipal Councils, such fines and penalties not to exceed $50 and costs in the following cases:—

Upon any person for the non-performance of his duties who has been elected to any office in the corporation and who neglects or refuses to accept such office unless good cause be shewn therefor, or to take the declaration of office and afterwards neglect the duties thereof.

For breach of any of the by-laws of the corporation.

There should be provided by a by-law of this kind, a proceeding to distrain in the event of the fines not being paid, and in the event of non-payment of fine or failure to collect by distress, imprisonment has to be provided for. The term of imprisonment (either with or without hard labor) is limited to 21 days. But in cities, and in the case of by-laws for the suppression of houses of ill-fame, the imprisonment may be made to extend to six months.

A by-law inflicting a larger fine or greater imprisonment than allowed, would be invalid, but a smaller fine or less imprisonment may be enacted.

Ornamental Trees.—Any Council may plant or bonus to the extent of 25 cents a tree the planting of trees on the highways or public squares. The

Ontario Government will recoup municipalities half the sums so expended. See "Ontario Tree Planting Act 1883," and Secs. 482 and 490 of Municipal Act 1883.

Temperance Laws.—For the passing of temperance laws, attention is directed to the Canada Temperance Act, better known as the Scott Act.

Seizing Bread.—A Council may pass a by-law for seizing and forfeiting bread and other articles of light weight and short measurement.

It has been recently decided that in such a by-law a Council may provide that each loaf should be stamped with the weight for which it is intended to be sold.

Supply of Water.—Contracts may be made with a company for supplying water for fire and other public purposes. The renting of hydrants or any other such contract must not be for more than ten years, with a provision of renewal for another ten years. A municipality may also purchase hydrants and fire apparatus and appliances.

Apprehension of Criminals.—A reward may be offered and paid by any Council for the discovery, apprehension or conviction of any criminal or one suspected of being so, in the case of a flagrant crime having been committed.

Compensation for lands taken.—When real property is entered upon, taken or used by a corporation in exercise of any of its powers, it must make compensation therefor to the owner or occupier, and if the compensation be not mutually agreed upon, resort may be had to arbitration.

It has been recently decided that the compensation need not be made before the lands are entered upon.

Summary remedy if by-laws not obeyed.—In addition to the punishment by fine for infraction of by-laws as mentioned on page 123 the Municipal Act provides another summary remedy as follows:

"Whenever any Municipal Council has any authority to direct, by by-law or otherwise, that any matter or thing should be done by any person or corporation, such Council may also, by the same or another by-law, direct that in default of its being done by the person, such matter or thing shall be done at the expense of the person in default, and may recover the expense thereof with costs by action or distress; and in case of non-payment thereof, the same shall be recovered in like manner as municipal taxes."

DIVISION II.—POWERS OF COUNCILS OF TOWNSHIPS, CITIES, TOWNS AND INCORPORATED VILLAGES.

It will be observed that in this division counties are not included.

Polling sub-divisions may be made or changed from time to time. Whenever the electors in any ward, township or village exceed 200, then it is compulsory to make polling sub-divisions. There must never be more than 200 electors in any polling subdivision.

The polling subdivisions for Legislative Assembly and municipal elections must be the same except that the Council of every city, town or incorporated village may by by-law unite any two adjoining polling sub-divisions for municipal purposes.

Disqualifying Tax Defaulters.—As to this power see pages 44 and 45.

Billiard and Bagatelle Tables.—Power is given to these municipalities to license and regulate the use of billiard and bagatelle tables; this applies to where they are in a house or place of public entertainment or resort, and whether the tables are used or not. A license fee may be imposed, and the legislature has made no limit as to what fee a corporation may fix upon.

Victualling Houses.—The number of victualling houses (i. e. houses where refreshments, fruit, oysters, etc., are sold, to be eaten in the house) may be limited; also other places for reception, refreshment or entertainment of the public. A license fee of no more than $20 may be imposed.

Transient Traders.—A by-law may be passed by a Council to license, regulate and govern transient traders and other persons who occupy premises for a temporary period—whose names have not been entered on the Assessment Roll for income or personal property. It matters not whether the transient trader sells the goods himself or employs a licensed auctioneer, he is subject to being licensed.

Schools.—These municipalities may obtain real property for the erection of Public Schools.

Cemeteries.—These may be established either within or without the municipality, but no cemetery should be within a city, town or incorporated village. The by-law acquiring land for a cemetery should state that it is appropriated for a public cemetery and for no other purpose.

The land acquired for a cemetery by a municipality becomes part of the municipality which acquires it, though it is without the municipality. A by-law for this purpose cannot be repealed, but in cases where the ground has not been used for burials the municipality may dispose of it and acquire other ground instead.

The trustees of any burying ground may transfer or sell the same to a municipality.

A by-law may be passed for preventing the violation of cemeteries, graves, tombs, tombstones or vaults.

Cruelty to Animals.—A by-law may be passed to prevent cruelty to animals and the destruction of birds. Besides this special provision, the general law provides for the protection of animals.

Dogs.—Owing to the danger of hydrophobia, the Municipal Act provides for the restraining and regulating the running at large of dogs, and gives power to pass by-laws for this purpose as well as the power to impose a tax on the owners. The by-law may enact that dogs running at large contrary to the by-law may be killed.

There is a special Act (Rev. Stat. Ont. chap. 194) providing that each municipality shall levy an annual tax of $1.00 for every dog and $2.00 for every bitch. A County Council may declare by by-law that such tax shall not be levied, and upon a copy being transmitted to a clerk of a township such tax shall not be levied, unless the Township Council in its turn passes a by-law declaring the Act to be in force. It is the duty of assessors to enter on the roll opposite the name of any person owning a dog, the number owned or kept. The fund from these taxes is to be appropriated for the protection of sheep. Attention is directed to the statute itself for more fully understanding its provisions.

Fences.—The height and description of what may be lawful fences may be settled by these municipalities. Compensation may be awarded by a by-law to those putting up fences on highways for increased expenses in connection therewith. This has been done by some municipal corporations in regard to wire fences.

The same power extends to division fences. A corporation may determine how the cost of them is to be apportioned, and direct that amounts so apportioned may be recovered in the same way as penalties.

If there is no by-law as to these division fences, then the Act relating to line fences applies. To treat of this act fully would require a volume of itself. See Rev. Stat. Ont. chap. 198.

It may be enacted that barbed wire fences should be constructed so as to afford protection to persons or animals.

Fences may be ordered by by-law to be removed in winter when bordering on the highways, so as not to impede travel through causing snow drifts. Or a particular kind of fence may be prescribed. The owners are entitled to compensation.

Water courses.—Owners of lands may be compelled to erect and keep up water gates where fences cross an open drain or water course and persons be prevented from obstructing them.

Weeds.—The growth of Canada thistles and other weeds may, as far as a by-law can do it, be prevented, and their destruction provided for. An inspector may be appointed for this purpose.

Filth.—There may be a by-law to prevent any

dirt, filth, carcases of animals on any street, road, lane or highway.

Burning Stumps, Brush, etc.—By-laws may be passed:

1. For regulating the times during which stumps, woods, logs, trees, brush, straw, shavings or refuse may be set on fire or burned in the open air.

2. For prescribing precautions to be observed during such times.

3. And for preventing such fires being kindled at other times.

See Statutes of Ontario for 1878, page 264, for a Special Act providing for preserving the destruction of forests from fire.

Exhibitions, shows, etc.—Exhibitions of wax works, menageries, circuses and other such shows may be regulated and licenses required, the license fee not to exceed $100. Fines may be provided for infringement of by-laws for this purpose.

Licenses of this kind are not to be granted on days of the Provincial Exhibition, or of any Electoral District Agricultural Society to hold circuses, etc., either on the grounds of the Society or within 300 yards from the grounds.

Injuries to Property and Notices.—For the protection of shade trees it is provided that by-laws may be passed for preventing the injuring or destroying of trees or shrubs planted for shade, or ornamental trees; also the defacing of private or other property by printed or other notices, as well on the other hand, the pulling down or defacing of sign boards and notices. The general law also provides that parties doing this injury may be proceeded against as vagrants.

Gas and Water companies.—These companies may be authorized to lay down pipes, subject to such regulations as the Council see fit.

Stock may be taken in or money lent to these companies by a municipality, or their loans or debentures guaranteed. The electors' consent must be obtained. In such case the head of a corporation holding stock to the extent of $10,000 shall be *ex officio* a Director of the Company.

Public Morals.—These Councils may in regard to public morals pass by-laws for the following purposes:—

For preventing the sale or gift of intoxicating drink to a child, apprentice or servant without the consent of a parent, master or legal protector;

For preventing the posting of indecent placards, writings or pictures, or the writing of indecent words, or the making of indecent pictures, or drawings, on walls or fences in streets or public places;

For preventing vice, drunkenness, profane swearing, obscene, blasphemous or grossly insulting language, and other immorality and indecency;

For suppressing disorderly houses and houses of ill-fame;*

For preventing or regulating and licensing exhibitions held or kept for hire or profit, bowling alleys

---

*Forbidding landlords to rent houses for these purposes is an allowable provision in a by-law. But it would not be allowable in a by-law to suppress these houses, to order their destruction.

and other places of amusement ;*

For suppressing gambling houses, and for seizing and destroying faro-banks, *rouge et noir*, roulette tables, and other devices for gambling found therein ;†

For preventing horse racing ;

For restraining and punishing vagrants, mendicants and persons found drunk or disorderly in any street, highway or public place.

For preventing indecent public exposure of the person or other indecent exhibitions ;

With regard to these powers conferred on municipal councils, it may be said that the general law also provides in nearly all of the cases for their prevention.

Establishing Boundaries.—A by-law may be passed for procuring the necessary estimates and making the proper application for ascertaining and establishing the boundary lines of a municipality according to law in case the same has not been done ; and for erecting and providing for the preservation of the durable monuments required to be erected for evidencing the same.

These Councils may apply to the Government for a survey to be made. They may do so by resolution, either on their own motion, or on application from one half of the resident landholders to be affected by land-marks and monuments or marking boundaries of concessions, lots, etc. In carrying out a survey of this kind, the directions of the stat-

---
*Note the word " preventing" as well as the words "regulating and licensing."

†See previous note as to houses of ill-fame.

ate have to be carefully followed, as otherwise the survey will be unauthorized. Thus, where it was shown that the application was made not by one-half of the resident landholders, but by ten freeholders, over half of whom had no deeds for their lands, and that eleven or twelve freeholders who would be affected by the survey were not parties to the application the survey was held unauthorized.

The expenses of the survey are paid by the County Treasurer on the certificate and order of the Commissioner of Crown Lands.

Pounds.—By Laws may be passed:—

(1) For providing sufficient yards and enclosures for the safe keeping of such animals as it may be the duty of the pound-keeper to impound.

(2) For restraining and regulating the running at large or trespassing of any animals, and providing for impounding them; and for causing them to be sold in case they are not claimed within a reasonable time, or in case the damages, fines and expenses are not paid according to law;

(3) For appraising the damages to be paid by the owners of animals impounded for trespassing contrary to the laws of Ontario or of the Municipality.

(4) For determining the compensation to be allowed for services rendered, in carrying out the provisions of any Act, with respect to animals impounded or distrained and detained in the possession of the distrainer.

The pound-keepers must take what animals are brought to him, but he is not liable if the animals have been taken wrongfully. But he must see that in exercising his duties that the formalities required by the statute and by-law as to notice, etc., are followed. There is a special statute relating to pound-keepers,—Rev. Stat. Ont. chap. 195.

Public Health.—Councillors are *ex-officio* health officers. It is specially incumbent on the head of the Council to see after this important matter. See page 74. A Health Committee may be appointed, to include, besides members of the Council, others who are not so.

The Act respecting the Public Health (Rev. Stat. Ont. chap. 190) gives large powers to Health officers. They may enter and examine any premises; may order the cleaning of the same; may destroy whatever in their opinion is necessary to be destroyed for the preservation of the public health; may, under certain circumstances, remove persons infected with a dangerously infectious disease.

A local Board of Health may be appointed by a Council, and in default of their appointing it, the Government may do so.

Tavern and Shop Licenses.—The question as to whether the Dominion or provinces respectively have the right of regulating liquor licenses has recently been the subject of much public discussion, and has also been before the courts. The provinces have exercised power in regard to them, although a Dominion License Act was passed in the session of 1883, which was enacted to come into force commencing with the year 1884. As, owing to the recent decision in the well-known case of *Regina* v. *Hodge,* it is likely that the provinces will continue to exercise the jurisdiction in regard to licenses, which it has heretofore exercised, we will here mention the powers conferred on municipalities by the Liquor License Act of Ontario. These powers are vested in Cities, Towns, Townships and Villages.

The Councils of these municipalities may by bylaw passed before the 1st March in any year limit the number of tavern licenses to be issued for the then ensuing license year, beginning on the 1st May. The by-law may apply also to future license years, if expressed so to be.

The License Act provides elsewhere (section 15) that licenses are at all events to be limited on the following scale:—In cities, towns and incorporated villages, one for each full 250 of the first 1,000 of the population and one for each full 400 over 1,000 of the population. Thus a town with a population of 5,300 would have 14 liquor licenses, calculated as follows:—

First	1,000—divided by 250		4
Then take 4000	" " 400		10
			14

And as to the remainder (300) being not equal to a full 400, there would not be an additional license.*

Municipalities can, as above mentioned, lessen, but not increase, this scale. License Commissioners have a somewhat similar power. When a municipality passes a by-law of this kind, a certified copy of the by-law must be sent immediately to the License Commissioners of the District.

There is also power vested in councils of cities and towns to pass by-laws to *add* to the accommodation required of taverns or houses of entertainment.

---

*In incorporated villages which are county towns the limit may be five in number. There is also a special provision as to the town of Clifton, excluding three hotels near the Falls of Niagara from the usual limit.

Shop licenses may also be limited by cities, towns, villages or townships by by-law passed before the 1st March, and by by-law passed before this date, the Councils of these municipalities may restrict persons holding shop liquor licenses to confine the business solely and exclusively to the selling of liquor, or may impose any restrictions upon the mode of carrying on such traffic as the Council may think fit.

The license fees are apportioned one-third to the province, two-thirds to each municipality.

Any municipality may by by-laws passed before the 1st March require a larger fee, than required by the Act, and the increase goes altogether to the municipality. But they cannot make the fee more than $200 except with the assent of the electors.*

A Municipal Council can not make the sum payable for a license vary according to locality. Thus where a township passed a by-law that in certain places the fees should be $100, and elsewhere $75, it was held by the court to be bad.

Whenever a by-law relating to licenses in any of the above cases is passed by a Council, a certified copy must be sent immediately to the License Commissioners.

DIVISION III.—POWERS OF COUNCILS OF COUNTIES AND CITIES.

Horse Thieves.—Councils of counties and cities

---

*The ordinary license fees are as follows:

Wholesale licenses,			$150 00
Tavern or shop licenses in cities			100 00
"	"	towns,	80 00
"	"	other municipalities,	60 00
Vessel license,			100 00

have not only the power, but are required to pass a by-law to provide that a sum not less than $20.00 shall be payable as a reward to those who pursue and apprehend any person or persons guilty of stealing a horse or mare within the county or city.

The reward is payable on the conviction of the thief, on the order of the judge before whom the conviction is obtained.

DIVISION IV.—POWERS OF COUNCILS OF COUNTIES, CITIES AND SEPARATED TOWNS.

Villages and townships, it will be observed are excluded.

Engineers, Inspectors, Gaol Surgeons, etc.—These Councils may appoint Engineers and also one or more Inspectors of the House of Industry. Surgeons of the Gaol, and other institutions under the charge of the municipality. And they may remove them.

Auctioneers.—They may license, regulate and govern auctioneers and other persons selling or putting up for sale good, wares, merchandise or effects by public auction. They may fix the fee for licenses and the time they are to be in force.

It would seem that they have the power to prevent auction sales on the public streets.

Auction sales of land do not require a license.

Hawkers and Peddlars.—People who are not permanent residents in the county, city or town, may under a by-law for the purpose, be required to take out a license for hawking or peddling goods carried about with them for sale.

This does not apply to persons not having the goods with them, who are merely soliciting orders.

Ferries.—Ferries between two places in one municipality may be licensed and regulated by by-law. The rates of ferriage may also be established The Ontario Government must sanction the by-law. As to ferries not between two places in the same municipality, they are within the exclusive jurisdiction of the Government.

Lands for High Schools.—They may obtain lands for High School purposes, and erect, preserve improve and repair the schools. The property may be disposed of when no longer required.

High Schools may be aided from the funds of the municipality.

Supporting Pupils at University and High Schools.—There is a special provision empowering them to make provision for supporting deserving pupils of the High Schools at the University at Toronto, the Upper Canada College and the Royal Grammar School in Toronto, also of aiding public school pupils at the High school This would apply to separate school pupils, it would seem.

Endowing Fellowships, etc.—Fellowships, scholarships, exhibitions and similar prizes in the University of Toronto, Upper Canada College and Royal Grammar School, Toronto may be endowed.

Public fairs.—On the petition of at least fifty qualified electors, these Councils may authorize the holding of public fairs at one or more of the most public and convenient places not separated from the municipality for municipal purposes.

These fairs are to be restricted to the sale, barter and exchange of cattle, horses, sheep, pigs and articles of agricultural production or requirement.

The by-law must establish rules and regulations for the government of the fairs, appoint a person to carry out these regulations and fix the fees to be paid him by persons attending the fair.

Public notice of the by-law must be given. The statute does not state what the notice must be as it does in other cases.

Junk stores.—Junk stores, or shops may be licensed and regulated and a license fee imposed for keeping them.

DIVISION V.—POWERS OF COUNCILS OF CITIES, TOWNS AND INCORPORATED VILLAGES.

It will be observed that counties and townships are excluded.

The Councils of every city, town and incorporated village may pass by-laws as follows :—

Water and Water Works.—For establishing, protecting and regulating public wells, reservoirs and other conveniences for the supply of water, and for making reasonable charges for the use thereof, and for preventing the wasting and fouling of public water;

For constructing, building, purchasing, improving, extending, holding, maintaining, managing and conducting water works and all buildings, materials, machinery and appurtenances thereto belonging in the municipality and neighborhood thereof, subject to the provisions contained in "*The Municipal Water works Act, 1882.*

They may prevent or regulate the erection or continuance of slaughter houses, gas works, tanneries, distilleries or other manufactories or trades which may prove nuisances; including the keeping of cattle and pigs, or swine, and cattle or cow-byres and piggeries.

A by-law declaring that "no person shall keep a slaughter house within the city *without the special resolution of the council,*" was held in the Court of Queen's Bench to be a void by-law as it permitted favoritism, and might be used in restraint of trade, or to grant a monopoly.

The ringing of bells, blowing, shouting and other unusual noises in streets and public places may be prevented. Likewise the firing of guns, etc., as well as fire-balls, squibs, crackers or fire-works. Charivaris and other like disturbances of the peace may also be prevented.

Vacant lots may be caused to be enclosed.

Driving upon sidewalks may be prevented.

Importuning travellers by hotel, vessel runners or cabmen may be prevented.

Public health.—By-laws may be passed to provide for the health of the municipality and against the spreading of contagious or infectious diseases.

Interments.—The interment of the dead may be regulated, and its taking place within the municipality prevented.

The keeping and returning of bills of mortality may be enforced.

Gunpowder.—The keeping and transporting of gunpowder, etc., may be regulated, magazines for storing it provided, and people compelled to store therein.

Preventing fires.—These Councils may act as follows :—

Appoint fire wardens, engineers and firemen, and promote, establish and regulate fire companies, hook and ladder companies, and property-saving companies;

Provide medals or rewards for persons who distinguish themselves at fires; and for granting pecuniary aid, or otherwise assist the widows and orphans of persons who are killed by accident at such fires;

Prevent or regulate the use of fire or lights in stables, cabinet makers' shops, carpenters' shops, and combustible places;

Prevent or regulate the carrying on of manufactories or trades dangerous in causing or promoting fire;

Prevent and remove or regulate the construction of any chimney, flue, fire-place, stove, oven, boiler or other apparatus or thing which may be dangerous in causing or promoting fire;

Regulate the construction of chimneys as to dimensions and otherwise, and enforce the proper cleaning of the same, and compel manufacturers and others to have such chimneys or other apparatus as shall consume the smoke or prevent the same from fouling the atmosphere or being carried by the wind or otherwise to other shops, houses or premises, to the inconvenience or injury of the neighboring premises or residents therein;

Regulate the mode of removal and safe keeping of ashes;

Regulate and enforce the erection of party walls;

Compel the owners and occupants of houses to have scuttles in the roof thereof, with approaches; or stairs or ladders leading to the roof;

Cause buildings and yards to be put in other respects into a safe condition to guard against fire or other dangerous risk or accident;

Require the inhabitants to provide so many fire buckets, in such manner and time as may be prescribed; and for regulating the examination of them, and the use of them at fires;

Authorize appointed officers to enter at all reasonable times upon any property subject to the regulations of the Council, in order to ascertain whether such regulations are obeyed, or to enforce or carry into effect the same;

Make regulations for suppressing fires, and for pulling down and demolishing adjacent buildings and other erections, when necessary to prevent the spread of fire;

Regulate the conduct and enforce the assistance of the inhabitants present at fires, and for the preservation of property at fires.

Removal of snow, ice and dirt.—Snow and ice may be required to be removed from the roofs of premises; snow, ice and dirt from the sidewalks, etc. In case of neglect of a person to remove after 24 hours' notice it may be provided that the removal be effected by the corporation at the expense of such person, and the expense charged as a special assessment against him. And persons neglecting to obey a by-law of this kind may be fined. A recent decision has declared this to be the law.

Obstruction of roads and streets by animals, vehicles, door-steps, porches, railings, etc., may be prevented or regulated by by-law.

Numbering Houses and Lots.—This may be done and the owner or occupant charged with the expense. The Council must keep a record of the streets and these numbers for public inspection.

Naming streets.—The boundary lines of streets, roads and other public communications may be surveyed, settled and marked by these municipalities and names given to them. The names may be affixed to the corners of streets on either public or private property.

No by-law for altering the name of any street, road, square, etc., is to have any force or effect until the by-law is registered in the Registry office.

Levels of cellars—Plans.—They may ascertain the levels of cellars already dug or to be dug, and compel them to be with reference to a line fixed by the by-laws. Block plans of buildings with the levels of the cellars and basements thereof may be required under a by-law before the erection of such buildings.

Sewerage and Drainage.—The construction of cellars, sinks, water closets, privies and privy vaults and the manner of draining the same may be regulated.

The Councils may compel or regulate the filling up, draining, cleaning, altering, relaying or repairing of any grounds, yards, vacant lots, cellars, private drains, sinks, cess-pools and privies; and assess the owners or occupiers of such grounds or yards, etc., with the cost thereof if done by the Council, on the default of the owners.

This power applies to sewers already constructed as well as those to be constructed.

Such other regulations as may be necessary for sanitary purposes may be made.

Rent may be charged for common sewers to people using them.

By a recent provision power is given to cities, towns or villages to acquire lands outside its own limits for drainage purposes, the consent of the outside municipality to be obtained, however, before the powers are exercised.

User of streets.—The conveyance of traffic in the public streets may be regulated and the width of the tires and the wheels of all vehicles.

It has been recently decided in the High Court that where by-laws were passed prescribing tires to be of a certain width, but the by-law was not to apply to any waggons conveying lumber or goods from a mill or manufactory distant more than two miles from the town limits, the by-law was illegal, as it discriminated against residents of the town in favor of others.

Cab stands.—Stands may be assigned for cabs and vehicles kept for hire; covered stands or booths may be erected on the streets, etc., but not on a sidewalk unless with the consent of the owner or lessee of the property fronting, abutting or adjoining the stand or booth.

Telegraph poles, etc.—The erection and maintenance of telegraph and telephone poles and wires may be regulated.

Children riding behind vehicles.—Children may be prevented from riding on the platform or behind waggons, etc., and provision made for preventing accidents arising from such causes.

Inspection of Milk, Meat, etc.—The inspection of milk, meat, poultry, fish and other natural products offered for sale for human food or drink may be provided for and inspectors appointed.

Free Libraries.—In 1882 a "*Free Libraries Act*" was passed authorizing cities, towns and villages to establish free libraries. See page 58 of statutes of

1882.

Markets, etc.—There has been recent legislation in regard to markets embodied in section 497 of the Municipal Act 1883 as follows:

"No municipality shall impose, levy or collect a market fee upon any wheat, barley, rye, corn, oats, or upon any grain, or upon any hay or other seed, or wool, lumber, lath, shingles, or cordwood or other firewood, or upon dressed hogs, or cheese, or upon hay, straw, or other fodder, that may be brought to market or to the market place for sale or other disposal, or upon the person bringing, or the vehicle in which the same is or shall be brought.

No market fee shall be charged, levied or imposed upon or in respect of butter, eggs or poultry brought to market, or upon the market place, for sale, unless a convenient and fit place in which to offer or expose the same for sale shall be provided by the Municipality, which shall afford shelter in summer, and shelter and reasonable protection from the cold in winter.

When the vendor of any article brought within the Municipality in pursuance of a prior contract for the sale thereof proceeds direct to the place of delivery thereof, under such contract, without hawking the same upon the streets or elsewhere within the Municipality, it shall not be lawful to impose, levy or collect a market fee thereon, or in respect thereof or on the vehicle in which the same is so brought.

Where there is no prior contract as mentioned in the previous sub-section, no market fee shall be imposed, levied or collected upon or in respect of any article brought into any Municipality after the hour of ten o'clock in the forenoon, nor on or in respect of any vehicle in which such article is so brought, unless such article is offered or exposed for sale upon the market place of such Municipality.

No by-law shall require hay, straw or other fodder to be weighed, or wood to be measured, where neither the vendor nor purchaser desire to have the same so weighed or measured.

After nine o'clock in the forenoon, between the first day

of April and the first day of November, and after ten o'clock in the forenoon, between the first day of November and the first day of April, no person shall be compelled to remain on any market place with any article which he may have been exposing or offering for sale in such market place, but may after the expiration of such hour, proceed to sell such article elsewhere than in or on said market place: Provided that such person has paid the market fee on or in respect of such article, or the vehicle in which the same is contained.

No market fees shall be imposed by any Municipality higher than those contained in the following scale:—

Upon articles brought to the market place in a vehicle drawn by two horses, upon which fees may be imposed, not more than............ ten cents.

Upon articles brought to the market place in a vehicle drawn by one horse, not more than five cents.

Upon articles brought to the market place by hand or in any basket or vessel, not more than..two cents.

Upon or in respect of live stock driven to or upon the market place for sale, as follows:—

Every horse, mare, or gelding, not more than ten cents.
Every head of horned cattle, not more than five cents.
Every sheep, calf, or swine, not more than two cents.

No fee shall be imposed or levied by any municipality for weighing or measuring greater than as follows:—

For weighing a load of hay.................fifteen cents.
For weighing slaughtered meat, or grain, or other articles exposed for sale, under one hundred pounds..two cents.
Over one hundred pounds, and up to one thousand pounds..five cents.
Over one thousand pounds.......................ten cents.
For weighing live animals, other than sheep or pigs, per head....................................three cents.
Sheep or pigs, if more than five, per head......one cent.
If less than five, for the lot.......................four cents.
For measuring a load of wood..................five cents.

Subject to the other provisions of this section, the Municipality may regulate the sale by retail in the public streets, or on vacant lots adjacent thereto, of any of the articles herein mentioned, and may regulate traffic in the streets, and prevent the blocking up of the same by vehicles or otherwise."

These provisions do not apply where there is a by-law in force allowing sale except at the market without payment of fees. Such a by-law may impose fees on persons voluntarily using the market, and on others taking advantage of the market by selling on a part of a street within 100 yards of the market place. Grain, seeds, dressed hogs and wool are an exception to this 100 yards rule. A by-law of this kind can not impose higher fees than what were in force 1st March, 1882.

When markets are made in or out of streets after 10th March, 1882, no fees can be charged on such markets.

Where there were no fees charged in a municipality on 10th March, 1882, such a by-law as is spoken of in the second preceding paragraph cannot be passed, and the provisions of section 497 above quoted will apply without being subject to change on the part of the municipality.

After 9 o'clock a. m. from 1st April to 1st November, and 10 o'clock a. m. from 1st November to 1st April, no person can be compelled to remain on a market with any produce or stuff he has for sale.

Every city, town and village council has power besides that of establishing markets to regulate those that are already established.

They can prevent and regulate the sale by retail in the public streets or vacant lots adjacent thereto of any meat, vegetables, grain, hay, fruit, beverages. small ware and other articles offered for sale; also the buying and selling of animals exposed for sale or marketed.

The selling and weighing of grain, meat, farm produce, small wares, etc., may be regulated ; criers and vendors of small wares may be prevented from practicing their calling in the market place, public street or vacant lots.

The sale of fresh meat may be licensed, and at license fee as high as $50 in cities and $25 in towns and villages imposed for selling it in less quantities than by the quarter carcas.

Forestalling of goods required for family use may be prevented, and hucksters, grocers, butchers and runners restricted in purchasing them.

The measuring of lime, laths, cordwood, coal and other fuel may be regulated.

Penalties may be imposed for light weight or short count or measurement in anything marketed.

It may be provided that butchers' meat distrained for rent of market stalls may be sold after six hours' notice.

The assize of bread may be regulated and the use of deleterious materials in making it, prevented ; the seizure and forfeiture of bread made contrary to the by-law may be also provided for. See page 124.

DIVISION VI.—POWERS OF COUNCILS OF CITIES AND TOWNS.

These urban municipalities may pass by-laws for the following purposes :—

Intelligence Offices.—These may be licensed for registering the names and residences of and giving information to or procuring servants for employers in want of domestics or laborers, and for registering the names and residences of and giving information to or procuring employment for domestics, servants and laborers. The municipality may fix the fees to be charged by the keepers.

These offices may be regulated, and the duration of the license fixed.

The license fee may be fixed as high as $10, and any Intelligence office kept without a license prohibited.

Wooden Buildings.—The regulation and erection of buildings and the prevention of wooden buildings or additions as well as of wooden fences in specified parts of the town provided for ; likewise the erection of buildings other than with main walls of brick, iron or stone, or roofing of incombustible material, within defined areas of the city or town may be prohibited. Any building constructed in contravention of the by-law may be authorized to be pulled down or removed.

Police.—As to Police see page 110. A superannuation and benefit fund for fire and police force may be provided for, as well as for their families.

Industrial Farm—Exhibitions.—Property may be acquired either within or without the city or town, or on the Industrial Farm for a public park garden or walk or for a public place-for exhibitions. Buildings may be erected and these places managed under the authority of the city or town.

Almshouses—charities.—One or more Almshouses or Houses of Refuge may be established within the city or town, or on the Industrial farm or Exhibition grounds. As will be seen above, these may be outside the city or town.

A Corporation surveyor, who must be a Provincial Land Surveyor may be appointed.

Gas and Water.—The municipality may itself construct gas and water works, and levy an annual special rate to defray the yearly interest of the expenditure for the works. There was a special Act passed in 1882, relating to water works. See Statutes of 1882, page 73. This Act also applies to villages.

Under the general municipal law it is required that a poll of the electors must declare in favor of the Waterworks by-law. The by-law must be passed within three months after holding the poll. In case the by-law is rejected no other by-law for the same purpose is to be submitted within the current year.

The management of waterworks is generally entrusted to a Board of Commissioners, who may be elected by the Council itself, but the general course adopted in cities is by virtue of special legislation to have the Board of Water Commissioners constituted and to have the members elected by the people. Reference is particularly directed to the Act of 1882 above spoken of.

DIVISION VII.—POWERS OF COUNCILS OF TOWNSHIPS, TOWNS AND VILLAGES.

Cities and counties are omitted.

The municipalities included in this division may borrow money and issue debentures for the purpose and subject to the provisions of *"The Ontario Tile, Stone and Timber Drainage Acts,"* which were passed in 1878 and 1880. See Act of 1878, page 52, and Act of 1880, page 15.

DIVISION VIII.—POWERS OF COUNCILS OF TOWNS AND INCORPORATED VILLAGES.

Towns and villages have the following powers:—

Licensing Vehicles.—To regulate and license the owners of livery stables and of horses, cabs, carriages, omnibuses and other vehicles for hire ; to establish the rates of fare to be taken by the owners or drivers and to enforce the payment thereof. See page 111.

DIVISION IX.—EXCLUSIVE POWERS OF COUNCILS OF COUNTIES.

Protecting Booms.—Booms on any stream or river may be protected and regulated, for the safe keeping of timber, saw logs and staves.

Guaranteeing Debentures.—The County Council may guarantee the debentures of any municipality within the county.

Livery Stables.—In a county, where there are county gravel or macadamized roads, under the jurisdiction and control of the county, supported by municipal taxation and free from toll, the County Council have power to pass by-laws (a) for regulating and licensing the owners of livery stables : (b) and of horses, cabs, carriages, omnibuses, and all other vehicles used or kept for hire : (d) for regulating the width of tires on such vehicles :* (e) for establishing the rates of fare that may be taken by owners or drivers : (f) for enforcing the payment of such licenses, regulating rates of fare for the conveyance of goods or passengers : (g) and for enforcing the width of tire that may be used on such vehicles when travelling on the aforesaid county gravel or macadamized roads.

Board of Audit—Criminal Justice, etc.—Every County Council must appoint at its first meeting

---

*Note that the power is restricted to "such vehicles" as are previously mentioned.

two members of the Board of Audit. Not more than one of them can belong to the Council. Their salary is not to be more than $4 per day and 5c mileage each way.

Improvements by either county of a Union.—The following provisions are an exception to the general rule that during the union of counties all laws applicable to counties shall apply to the union as if the same formed one county.

A Council of united counties may make appropriations and raise funds to enable either county separately to make improvements in such separate county.

On such a question none but the Reeves and Deputy-Reeves of the county to be affected, can vote, except that in the case of a tie the warden may vote, though he is not a representative from such county.

The united counties' Treasurer must pay over sums so raised without any deduction.

The property in the county affected is alone to be taxed for this purpose, and any debenture issued is to be issued as the debenture of this one county only. Such debenture, however, is to be under the seal of the united counties, and to be signed by the warden.

Support of destitute Insane Persons.—A County Council must make provision for the whole or partial support of such destitute insane persons as cannot be properly admitted to the provincial asylums. This must be done either in the county gaol or some other place within the county. The Council determine the sum to be paid for such support and also the parties to whom such sums shall be paid by the County Treasurer.

This is a new provision.

DIVISION X.—EXCLUSIVE POWERS OF COUNCILS OF TOWNSHIPS.

Statute Labor.—Statute labor may be commuted for no more than five years at not exceeding $1 for each days' labor. This applies both to residents and non-residents.*

Besides commutation for this period, it may be provided that not more than $1 may be accepted for each day's labor.

The number of days' labor may be increased or reduced. This is by a by-law operating generally and ratably.

The manner of performing the labor, and the township divisions where to be performed may be regulated.

Statute labor may be abolished by Townships

Town Hall.—Land may be acquired in any town or incorporated village either within or partly within the original boundaries of the township for the purpose of erecting, renting or acquiring a Town Hall. This gives power, it will be observed, to acquire land outside the corporation. Meetings, nominations, elections, posting of notices, assessment rolls, voters' lists, etc., or other acts are valid if done at such a Town Hall as if done within the township.

Obstructions to streams or Water courses.—The Township Council may pass by-laws to prevent the obstruction of streams, creeks and water courses by

---

*Non-residents are not compelled actually to do statute labor, but are subject as above stated, to assessment for commutation of statute labor.

Obstructions to streams or water courses.—The Township Council may pass by-laws to prevent the obstruction of streams, creeks and water courses by trees, brushwood, timber, etc.; also for clearing away and removing such obstructions at the expense of the offenders or otherwise. The amount of such expense may be levied in the same manner as taxes are levied. Penalties may be imposed on persons causing such obstructions.

When a stream in any township is cleared of obstructions notice in writing may be served on the Council of an adjoining municipality requiring them to clear the stream within their municipality. This other municipality must within six months remove all obstructions to the satisfaction of an inspector appointed by the County Council.

Registration of Plans.—The registration of sub-divisions of land in a township may be enforced where the survey or sub-division so differs from the original Crown survey that the parcel sold cannot be easily identified, the map or plan not having been registered. The expense in connection with this may be levied by a special rate on the lands comprised in the plan.

CHAPTER XI.
HIGHWAYS AND BRIDGES.

In regard to the important matter of highways and bridges, there are certain powers and duties imposed and conferred on all municipalities, while as to other powers and duties they are exclusively possessed by certain classes of municipalities. They are comprised in the statute in five divisions.

DIVISION I.—GENERAL PROVISIONS.

The following are to be deemed common and public highways:—

All allowances for roads made by Crown Surveyors.*

All roads laid out by virtue of any statute.

Any roads wherever the public money has been expended.

Any roads on which statute labor has been usually performed.

Any roads passing through the Indian lands, except where such roads have been already altered or may hereafter be altered according to law.

A by-law cannot be passed to take any lands of the Crown in addition to those appropriated by the Crown for the purpose of highways, so that the country may be opened up.

---
*This is made to extend to general surveys such as made by the Canada Company and other companies, etc.

If a highway has been used for many years, though it is not the correct highway as marked on the plan, it may be taken as the correct highway.

The law deals in a liberal spirit in regard to highways with a due regard to the customs and necessities of a new country where roads are in their infancy and much land unenclosed.

The spending of public money, spoken of on the previous page, means money of the Government or of the corporation.

Municipal Councils have conferred upon them the power and the duty of dealing with existing roads and opening up new ones. This does not include the roads of joint stock companies, unless acquired by the municipalities.

If road companies allow their road to be out of repair for nine months after the time fixed by arbitration for repair of the same, the company forfeits all right to the road, and it may be assumed by the county. If the county fail to do so within one month after the nine months, then the particular municipality which would, as explained in the following pages, be required to maintain it, would have this duty cast upon it.

In the case of a road company abandoning its road in whole or in part the same results follow as just pointed out.

But a company cannot abandon any *intermediate* portion of their road without a by-law of the County Council consenting thereto.

The same law applies to purchasers from the companies as well as to the companies.

Cities or towns may, with the consent of an adjacent municipality, acquire control over a public highway in such municipality for a public avenue or walk. They may also acquire from the owners of land sufficient to increase the road to the extent of 100 feet or less. See page 124 as to compensation.

County bridges may be assumed by villages in which the bridges are situated, the bridge to be toll free. The county and village are both to pass by-laws for the purpose. The village is to pay to the county part of the cost of construction.

Every public road, street, bridge and highway must be kept in repair by the corporation. The neglect of the corporation to repair subjects it to a fine, and damages may be recovered by persons injured. The action for damages must be brought within three months after the damages have been sustained.

A municipality which is required to keep a bridge in repair must also keep its approaches maintained for 100 feet from each end: the remaining portion of such approaches is to be maintained by the local municipality in which they are situated.

In general terms, non-repair may be said to be any defect in a highway which renders it unsafe for ordinary travel.

The nature of the country and the character of its roads and the care usually taken by the municipality are to be considered in determining what is a case of non-repair: a new township is not expected to have its roads as perfect in repair as one long settled.

Each case may be said to be governed by its own peculiar circumstances, such as the season of the year, the place of the accident, the hour of the day or night, and the manner and nature of the accident.

These questions are more questions of fact than of law, and are to be determined by a jury on a trial.

If a railing be necessary for the safety of passengers, the municipality must have it constructed.

In some cases, the existence of snow or ice in a dangerous state would constitute negligence in a corporation, in others not. There have been very many cases of this kind tried and it is hard to deduce from them a rule to govern all cases.

It is no defence for a corporation to say that the neglect was the fault of their servants, as an overseer of highways, for instance. It is responsible for the neglect of its servants.

A Councillor should, when a defect comes to his notice see to the repair, as its coming to his notice may affect the corporation's liability.

If the cost of rebuilding the road or making the necessary repair would exceed the statutable limit of taxation it may be that there would be no obligation to repair. But in such a case it is apprehended to be the duty of the corporation so to close up the road that there will be no danger in using it.

Though a corporation is bound to repair only its own highways, and not such roads as are laid out by private individuals, still, through long usage of the latter by the public, and their being maintained by the corporation, it may happen that the duty of keeping them in repair will be cast on the municipality.

The County Council have exclusive jurisdiction

over the following roads and bridges.

1. All roads and bridges lying *within* any township, town or village of the county, *and* which the Council of the County by by-law with the assent of the local municipality, assumes as a county road or bridge.

2. All bridges across streams separating two townships in the county.

3. All bridges crossing streams or rivers over one hundred feet in width, within the limits of any incorporated village in the county, and connecting any highway leading through the county.

4. All bridges over rivers forming or crossing boundary lines between two municipalities.'

It will be observed that the first class mentioned are expressly required to be assumed by by-law. Classes two and three it seems (though not so expressly mentioned in the part of the statute quoted) are also required to be assumed.

Any County Council may assume, make and maintain any township or county boundary line at the expense of the county, or may grant such sum or sums from time to time for the said purpose as they may deem expedient.

The boundary lines just mentioned include boundary lines between townships.

Roads or bridges in a township assumed by a county must, with as little delay as reasonably may be, be planked, gravelled or macadamized at the expense of the county, or the bridge be built in a good and substantial manner. See afterwards in this chapter the concluding part of Division IV. as to County Councils casting the burden of maintaining roads on local municipalities.

The County Council must cause to be built and maintained in like manner all bridges on any river or stream over 100 feet in width within the limits of any incorporated village in the county "necessary to connect any public highway leading through the county."

It is the duty of County Councils to erect and maintain bridges over rivers forming or crossing boundary lines between two municipalities within the county. This does not apply to the case of a city or separated town.

What is meant by a "river" has sometimes occasioned disputes. It has been decided in the Court of Appeal that a stream called the Black Creek in the County of Perth, which is from thirty to forty feet wide with well defined banks, is a river.

Even where there is what is indisputably a river, the County Council has some discretion as to the place where the bridge should be erected, and must be allowed to some extent to judge of the necessity of the erection.

Where a County had maintained a bridge but had not by by-law assumed it, it was held that it was not compelled to maintain the bridge.

A bridge should be constructed in such a way as not to be a public nuisance.

In the case of a bridge over a river forming or crossing a boundary line between two counties or a county and city, such bridge must be erected and maintained by the councils of the counties or county and city respectively. In case they do not agree as to the proportion of expense the matter is to be settled by arbitration. See Chapter VI". "Arbitrations" page 106.

All township boundary lines not assumed by the County Council must be opened, maintained and improved by the township councils, except where it is necessary to erect or maintain bridges over rivers forming or crossing boundary lines between two municipalities.

The same law applies where township boundaries happen to be also county boundaries.

Where roads are between two municipalities, they have joint jurisdiction, except as in the case of bridges as has been mentioned before in this chapter, where they are under county jurisdiction, or the jurisdiction of two counties in the case of boundary lines between counties.

Both Councils must concur in by-laws respecting these roads.

If they do not concur, there must be arbitration. This arbitration is to take place when one Council fails to pass a by-law within six months of the other, and receives notice from the first Council of the by-law having been passed. The best way of giving notice is to attach a copy of the by-law to the notice.

Although no Provincial, Ordnance or Dominion road or bridge can be interfered with by a municipality, still a Provincial proclamation may pass a road or bridge of the province under the control of the municipality. The consent of the Dominion may be obtained to a municipality passing a by-law in relation to Ordnance or Dominion roads; the by-law must recite such consent, otherwise it will not be valid.

When a Council closes a road, any person who will be excluded from ingress and egress to his land or residence is entitled, besides compensation, to compel the Council to provide some other convenient road or way of access to his land or residence. Without this, the road cannot be stopped.

A road or street must not be laid out more than 100 feet nor less than 66 feet wide, except where an existing road or street is widened. A local municipality may lay out roads or streets differently with the consent of the County Council.

A by-law opening up a road should recite the width of it, and should show its particular course.

Any road, when altered, may be of the same width as formerly.

An owner of land may with the consent of the Municipal Council lay out a highway or street less than sixty-six feet.

In the case of
(a) stopping up;
(b) altering;
(c) widening;
(d) diverting
(e) or selling

any *original allowance* for road, or
(a) establishing;
(b) opening;
(c) stopping up;
(d) altering;
(e) widening;
(f) diverting;
(g) or selling

any *other* public highway, road, street or lane, written or printed notices of the intended by-law must be posted up one month previously in six of the most public places in the immediate neighborhood of such original allowance for road, street or other highway, road, street or lane.

This notice must also be published weekly for at least four successive weeks in some newspaper (if there be any) in the municipality; and in either case in the county town, if any such newspaper there be.

The Council must also previously hear in person or by counsel or attorney any one whose land might be prejudicially affected thereby, and who petitions to be heard.

The petitioners for the by-law are to pay the expenses attendant on such notices being given; upon payment of these expenses, the clerk is to give the notices.

By-laws under which roads are opened on private property must be registered to give them effect.

In the case of disputes concerning roads, etc., the head of the Council has power in an investigation to administer an oath or affirmation.

DIVISION II.—POWERS OF COUNTIES, TOWNSHIPS, CITIES, TOWNS AND INCORPORATED VILLAGES IN RELATION TO ROADS AND BRIDGES.

Under this heading, it will be noticed, all municipalities are included.

These municipalities may pass by-laws for
1. Opening;
2. Making;
3. Preserving;
4. Improving;
5. Repairing;
6. Widening;
7. Altering;
8. Diverting;
9. Stopping,—

roads, streets, squares, alleys, lanes, bridges or other public communications.

It will be observed that *levelling, raising* or *lowering* streets are not mentioned here. When a municipality either levels, raises or lowers a street, then comes the question whether it should compensate the owner of land whose property would be injured thereby. It has been decided that they must do so.

Municipalities have also power to remove any obstructions upon roads and bridges, and can permit sub-ways for cattle under a highways.

Roads can be made across railway lands, but subject to certain restrictions.

The collection of tolls is restricted to what may be necessary "to defray the expense of making or repairing." See page 156 as to tolls on county bridges assumed by villages.

Regulations may be made as to pits, precipices and deep waters, and other places dangerous to travellors. It may be said that protection must be made to save corporations from actions for damages.

In regard to road allowances, timber, trees, stone, sand or gravel may be preserved or sold by municipalities.

The Crown may now also grant timber licenses on road allowances. but in the event of their doing so, the municipality is entitled to a portion of the timber dues. See Rev. Stat. Ont. Cap. 26.

In selling a road allowance (whether an unused road or one that has been stopped up) the parties next adjoining whose lands the same is situated have the right of pre-emption. It must first be offered to them, and in case they refuse to purchase for such price as the Council thinks reasonable then the sale may be made to any other person at a greater price.

The closing up of a road allowance is one thing, the selling and conveying it, another. The former must be done before the latter takes place, nor is there any compulsion to sell, but when the sale does take place, the requisites in the preceding paragraph mentioned, are necessary.

When a road is substituted for an original allowance without compensation to a person whose land is taken, such person, if he owns land adjoining, is entitled to the original road. A conveyance may be made by the corporation on a report in writing of its Surveyor or of a Deputy-Provincial Land Surveyor that the new or travelled road is sufficient for a public highway. The surveyor should state in his report the width of the new road and the line to be run.

When an original road allowance is useless to the public and lies between lands owned by different parties, the Council may sell a part to such parties. In case compensation was not paid for the new road, and the person through whose land it runs does not own the land adjoining the original road allowance, the amount received from the purchaser of the old road allowance is to be paid to the person who owned the new road.

When a by-law is to be passed for opening up an original road allowance, notice in writing must be given to the person in possession at least eight days before the meeting of the Council.

A municipality can grant aid to an adjoining municipality for making, opening, etc., any highway, road, street, bridge or communication passing from or through an adjoining municipality.

A municipality may search for and take timber, gravel, stone or other material necessary for road-work. In the event of dispute, the right of entry and the price or damage is to be settled by arbitration.

DIVISION III.—POWERS OF TOWNSHIPS, CITIES, TOWNS AND VILLAGES IN RELATION TO ROADS AND BRIDGES.

Counties, it will be noticed, are not included in this division.

Those municipalities may grant aid to counties either by loan or otherwise, in making new roads and bridges.

They may also enter into a joint arrangement with one another (if in the same county or united counties) for executing any work in their jurisdiction at their joint expense and for their joint benefit.

Before a by-law for this purpose is passed the arrangement should be completed.

If any Township Council fails to perform its duty in maintaining township boundary lines in the same way as other township roads, the County Council may, on petition from the interested townships enforce joint action on the Township Councils. Or the resident ratepayers bordering on such lines may make the petition.

To act on either kind of petition the County Council may*:—

1. Determine the amount which each Township Council interested shall be required to apply for the opening or repairing of such lines of road.

---

*The action is not compulsory; it is permissive as far as the County Council is concerned.

2. Direct the expenditure of a certain portion of statute labor.

3. Or both.

as may seem necessary.

The County Council appoint a Commissioner or Commissioners to enforce their orders. If the representatives of any of the townships intimate their intention to execute the work, the Commissioner or Commissioners must delay proceedings for a reasonable time. If the work is not then proceeded with during the favorable season, then the commissioners are to undertake and finish it themselves.

The sums to be paid by townships, which are determined by the County treasurer on the order of commissioners, and the amount retained out of township moneys in his hands. If there are not any such moneys before the striking of a county rate, an additional rate must be levied by the County Council against such township.

When the townships are in different counties, the respective wardens are made the arbitrators, the county judge of the county in which lies the township first making the application being the third arbitrator.

The warden of the county in which the township lies is the convener of the meeting. He must notify the other two within eight days of receiving the application, the meeting to take place within twenty-one days from the application.

The arbitrators or any two of them determine the share of work to be borne by the respective townships, and also appoint a commissioner or commissioners to superintend such work.

Path-masters must obey the commissioners.

DIVISION IV.—POWERS OF COUNTY COUNCILS IN RELATION TO ROADS AND BRIDGES.

Any county original road allowance, not within a city, town or village, may be stopped up or stopped up *and* sold. See page 161 as to notice required to be given.

County Councils may pass by-laws for :—

1. Opening;
2. Making;
3. Preserving;
4. Improving;   Roads, streets, squares, alleys, lanes, bridges or other public communications.
5. Repairing;
6. Widening;
7. Altering;
8. Diverting;
9. Stopping up;

1. Within one or more Townships.
2. Between two or more Townships.
3. Any bridge across rivers over 100 feet in width within any Incorporated Village in the County, connecting any public highway leading through the County, and which is a continuation of a County road or between the County and any adjoining County or City, separated Town or Incorporated Village within the boundaries of the County, as the interests of the inhabitants of County in the opinion of Council, require to be opened, made, preserved and improved.
4. For entering upon, breaking up, taking or using any land in any way necessary or convenient for the said purposes, subject to the restrictions in the Act contained.

With regard to trees obstructing highways, the

Council may direct trees to be cleared on each side of the highways for a space not exceeding 25 feet by the proprietor. A time is to be appointed in the by-law for the purpose, the county Surveyor to do it, in case of default. Authority may be given to the overseer or other officer to use the trees for the improvement of roads and bridges, or that he may sell them to defray the expenses of the work; the Council may further pay such expenses out of the county funds.

Double tracks, in snow roads, may be provided for.

Town, township or village may be aided (where the Council deem the county at large sufficiently interested in the work) in the making of roads and bridges. The debentures of the local municipalities may be guaranteed.

The County Council may require the whole or any part of a county road within any local municipality shall be opened, improved and maintained by such local municipality.

As to sale or lease of mineral rights on or under roads see page 169.

DIVISION V.—POWERS OF TOWNSHIP COUNCILS IN RELATION TO ROADS AND BRIDGES.

A Township Council may aid an adjoining county in

1. Making;
2. Opening;
3. Maintaining;
4. Widening;
5. Raising;
6. Lowering;
7. Or otherwise improving;

Any highway, road, street, bridge or communication lying *between* the Township and any other Municipality.

Aid may also be granted to the county in which the township lies for the same purpose when the road, etc., is "assumed by the county as a county work or agreed to be assumed *on condition of such grant.*"

A township may stop up, lease or sell an original road allowance. See page 161 as to notice required to be given. Besides the notice the by-law of the township must be confirmed by a by-law of the County Council at the ordinary session of the County Council, held not sooner than three months, nor later than one year next after the passing thereof."

With regard to trees obstructing highways, Township Councils have the same power as to their highways, as is possessed by the County Council. See page 167.

They may set apart as much of *any* highway as they may deem necessary for the purposes of a footpath; they may provide for the imposition of penalties on persons travelling thereon on horseback or in vehicles.

Any township or county may sell or lease by public auction or otherwise, the right to take minerals on or under their roads. Notice of the by-law authorizing such lease or sale must be posted up in six of the most public places in the immediate neighborhood at least one month previous to the time fixed for considering such by-law.

In the sale or lease, the purchaser or lessee must be restrained from interfering with the public travel.

In case the Trustees of any Police Village, or 15 of the inhabitant householders of any other unincorporated village or hamlet consisting of not less than 20 dwelling houses standing within an area of 200 acres, petition the Council of the township in which the village or hamlet is situate, and in case the petition of such unincorporated village or hamlet, not being a police village, is accompanied by a certificate from the registrar of the county within which it lies, that a plan of the village or hamlet has been duly deposited in his office according to the registry laws, the Council may pass a by-law to stop up, sell and convey, or otherwise deal with any original allowance for road lying within the limits of the village or hamlet, as the same shall be laid down on the plan, but subject to all the restrictions with reference to the sale of original road allowances.

When a village is partly in each of two townships, whether in the same county or not, each township has the power (as to the subject just mentioned) to deal with such parts as is situate within its limits.

A Township Council can provide for the performance of statute labor upon the roads of their township to the extent of the commutation tax charged in respect of non-resident lands and for the payment thereof out of the general funds of the municipality before such tax has been received from the county treasurer; the performance of such work is not necessarily restricted to any particular statute labor division.

CHAPTER XII.
DRAINAGE AND OTHER LOCAL IMPROVEMENTS.

The municipal law relating to drainage and other local improvements has received much development of late years. There has been a great deal of legislation in regard to it, and it has frequently come before the courts.

Under this head the powers and duties conferred and imposed on municipalities are comprised in four divisions.

DIVISION I.—TOWNSHIPS, CITIES AND VILLAGES.

Municipal Councils may pass by-laws for deepening and straightening streams, etc., or draining or removing obstructions preventing the free flow of water, or lowering the waters of any lake or pond for the purpose of reclaiming flooded land or more easily draining any lands.

The following requisites for the passing of a by-law for any of these purposes are necessary.

1. The majority* in number of the persons as shewn by the last revised assessment roll to be the owners (resident or non-resident) of the property to be benefited must make a petition for the purpose.

---

*The work of embanking, pumping or other mechanical operations requires more than a majority; it is specially provided that two thirds of the owners must petition. This kind of work may be maintained continually, and full power is given to defray the annual cost

2. An examination of the work must be made by an engineer or surveyor.

3. He must make plans and estimates of the work, and assess the real property to be benefited, stating, as nearly as may be, in his opinion, the proportion of benefit to be derived by every road and lot or portion of lot.

Although land benefited is not mentioned in a petition, it has been decided that if the surveyor reports that such land would be benefited and the owner is accordingly assessed, the by-law is good.

But a Council has no power to authorize the undertaking of any work than the particular kind of work bargained for, and if that is impracticable or too costly they must refuse the petition.

Petitioners have a right to withdraw after signing, if they do so before the contract is let or the debentures are negotiated. So, if there does not remain a majority, the by-law is bad.

What constitutes a majority in a part of a township often forms a question of difficulty. No safe rule can be laid down except to secure a majority of those benefited or burthened.

Funds may be borrowed, or debentures issued for the cost of work and of arbitration. The debentures must not be less than $100 each, bearing interest not less than five per cent. and be payable within 15 years from date.

The Council, by a resolution subsequent to the by-law, may authorize the interest being included in the debentures instead of the interest being payable annually.

The cost of the works and the expenses of arbitration, publishing by-laws, etc., are to be included in the amount to be raised by the local rate.

Before the debentures are issued, any person may pay the amount of his assessment, less the interest. The debentures are then to be reduced proportionately.

Cases of complaint come before the Court of Revision, with right of appeal to the County Judge. The Court of Revision must sit not earlier than 20, nor later than 30 days from the day on which the by-law was first published, notice of which must be published with the by-law during the first three weeks of its publication.

The engineer or surveyor, in his assessment, need not confine it to the part of a lot actually drained, but may make it on the whole lot, on the half, or quarter, or other part owned by the one owner.

The proportion of benefit to be derived from any works by any parcels of land or roads may be shewn by the engineer or surveyor by placing sums of money opposite such parcels and roads; it is not necessary to state the fraction of the cost to be borne by each parcel or road.

There is a form of by-law given in the statute which must be followed. It is too long to be given here. See Statutes of 1883 chap. 18 sec. 571.

In the event of the assessment being altered by the Court of Revision or Judge, the by-law shall, before being finally passed, be amended so as to correspond with such alteration by the Court of Revision or Judge.

Before the final passing of the by-law it must be published once or oftener in every week for four weeks in such newspaper published either within the municipality or in the County Town or in a public newspaper published in an adjoining local municipality, as the Council may designate by resolution. There must also be published with it a notice of which the following may be taken as a form;

"Take notice that the following is a true copy of a by-law which will be taken into consideration by the Municipal Council of the township of after four weeks from the first publication thereof in the being the newspaper fixed upon by resolution of the said Council for the publication of this by-law and notice, the date of which first publication is day, the day of A. D. 188 (*if votes of electors required, as to which see latter part of this chapter add*,—and that the votes of the duly qualified electors in that behalf will be taken on day, the day of A. D. 188 , between the hours of nine o'clock in forenoon and five o'clock in the afternoon at the places mentioned in and fixed by the paragraph of the said above copy of the said proposed by-law) and any one intending to have such by-law or any part thereof quashed, must within ten days after the final passing thereof, serve a notice in writing upon the Reeve and the Clerk of the said Township of his intention to make application for that purpose to the High Court of Justice at Toronto during the sittings next ensuing the final passing of the by-law.

Dated the day of A. D. 188

A. B.

Township Clerk."

Instead of being published in a newspaper the Council may direct by *resolution* that a copy of the by-law and notice be served on each of several owners, their lessees or occupants, or upon the agent or agents of such owners or be left at their places of residence with some grown-up member of the family, or when the land is unoccupied and the owner and his agent is not a resident may send the copy by registered letter to the last known address. The by-law is not to be finally passed until after the expiration of three weeks from the last of such services.

The clerk must keep on file in his office a statutory declaration proving the service. The form of declaration may be as follows:—

I, A.B., of the   of   in the County of   (*occupation*) do solemnly declare.

That I did on   day the   day of   A.D. 188 , . serve C.D., the owner (or *as the case may be*) of lot   in the   concession of the Township of   with a true copy of the annexed by-law and notice by delivering the same to and leaving the same with the said C.D. at   (or by mailing the same in a registered letter addressed as follows:—"   " the registration certificate of which is hereto annexed)

And I make this solemn declaration conscientiously believing the same to be true and by virtue of the Act passed in the thirty-seventh year of Her Majesty's reign, intituled "An Act for the suppression of voluntary and extra Judicial oaths."

Declared before me at   in the County of   this   day of   A.D. 188   } A. B.

A Commissioner, &c.

The Council has power to amend the by-law when no sufficient means is provided for the completion of the work.

The work may be extended beyond the limits of the municipality in which the work was commenced.

Lands in an adjoining municipality or the road of a road company may be charged though the works are not carried into such adjoining municipality. The engineer or surveyor may assess such lands or roads if he thinks that they are benefited.

The engineer or surveyor determines and reports to the Council by which he was employed, whether the works shall be constructed and maintained solely at the expense of such municipality, or at the expense of both municipalities, and he also determines the proportion.

The Council of the municipality wherein the work is to be begun must notify the municipality to be benefited, and the municipality so notified is required to raise the necessary amounts.

There is provision for an appeal from the surveyor's report. This appeal is in the nature of an arbitration. It must be made within 20 days from the time the report is served.

This time may be extended, under certain circumstances on application to the County Judge.

Neither an engineer or surveyor who has been employed to make the survey, plans, etc., nor any interested ratepayer can be an arbitrator.

As to the arbitration generally see chapter on "Arbitrations."

When work has been *constructed* out of the general funds of the municipality prior to 10th February, 1876, the Council may, (without petition) on the report of an engineer or surveyor pass a by-law to charge the *maintenance* and *keeping in repair*, on the property benefited. This assessment may from time to time be changed on the report of the engineer or surveyor.

Any party wilfully placing obstructions in drains may be charged with the cost of removal of same and with 10 per cent addition. This may be assessed against his property.

If any dispute arises

(*a*) between individuals,

(*b*) between individuals and a municipality or company,

(*c*) between a company and municipality.

(*d*) or between municipalities

there is provision made for arbitration.

Damages recovered against a corporation for damage caused by drainage are to be charged on lands liable for cost of drainage.

Where a ditch is being constructed for drainage purposes along a road allowance, the earth taken from the ditch may be spread on the road. If the roads are timbered or stumps are in the way, they may be removed; not less than twelve feet of the centre of the road must be grubbed before the earth is spread upon it.

Provision is made for the construction of ditches on town lines between municipalities. In case of a petition being presented to any municipality for the making of a ditch, it may construct the ditch on either side of the road, and charge the adjoining municipality with the cost. Disputes are to be settled by arbitration. With reference to such ditch the other rules referred to throughout this chapter also apply.

The County Council may pass a by-law to deal with drainage where more than one municipality is affected. The county is to raise the necessary funds, but the townships are to be liable to the county for the same.

There is also provision for the construction of works in several counties.

In case ten property owners within ten days of the necessary publication of a report of Council, petition the Council not to proceed with the work, then a vote of the electors must be taken on the by-law.

The form of oath that may be required from a voter in such an election is as follows:—

You swear that you are of the full age of 21 years, and a natural born (*or* naturalized) subject of Her Majesty.

That you have not voted before in the township on the question now being voted upon.

That you are the owner (*or as the case may be*) of the land in respect of which you claim to vote, namely (*here mention the lands*).

That you are, according to law, entitled to vote on the said question.

That you have not, directly or indirectly, received any reward or gift, nor do you expect to receive any, for the vote which you tender.

That you have not received anything, nor has anything been promised to you, directly or indirectly, either to induce you to vote on the said question, or for loss of time, travelling expenses, hire of team, or any other service connected therewith.

That you have not directly or indirectly, paid or promised anything to any person, either to induce him to vote or refrain from voting.

So help you God.

The provisions just mentioned are recently enacted and are contained in the Municipal Act of 1883, sections 600 to 611. Among these, it is provided that minor municipalities may appear on the arbitration.

DIVISION II.—LOCAL IMPROVEMENTS IN CITIES, TOWNS AND VILLAGES.

A city, town or incorporated village may pass by-laws for ascertaining the real property to be benefited by a local improvement, and determining the proportions of assessment.

An appeal may be made to the Judge of the county court.

Special rates for local improvements apply to the following cases:

1. Making,
2. Enlarging,
3. Prolonging,
} *any* common sewer.

1. Opening,
2. Widening,
3. Prolonging,
4. Altering,
5. Macadamizing,
6. Grading,
7. Levelling,
8. Paving,
9. Planking.
} *any* street, lane, alley, public way, place, sidewalk, or any bridge forming part of a highway therein.

1. Curbing,
2. Sodding,
3. Planting,
} *any* street, lane, alley, square, or other public place.

and

Reconstructing as well as constructing any of these works.

Two-thirds in number representing. one-half in value of the property to be immediately benefited must petition for the local improvements.

Local improvement rates do not apply to any work of ordinary repair or maintenance, and local improvements are kept in repair out of the general funds.

The rate must be according to the frontage.

The notice of the proposed assessment must be published in two local newspapers; if there are not two, then in a newspaper nearest to the proposed improvement. The publication is to be once in each week for two weeks.

If a majority of the owners interested petition the Council against the assessment within one month after the last publication, no second notice of assessment for the same improvement can be given by the Council within two years thereafter.

In case the first assessment prove insufficient, further assessments may be made until sufficient shall be raised.

The assessment may be commuted with the parties liable for the rate.

If funds are furnished by the parties interested, the Council may do the work.

As to common sewers having a sectional area of more than four feet, the Council must, before the work is undertaken, provide one-third the cost by by-law for borrowing money.

Corner lots, triangular pieces of land, etc., may be specially provided for by by-law so as to provide an equitable mode of assessment for local improvements.

Lands unfit for building purposes are made special cases.

The cost of bridges and culverts may be laid on other property benefited in a particular locality, other than the lands fronting on the bridges or culverts.

The Council may permit owners to improve sidewalks in front of their lands. As long as they keep them in repair, they are not liable for the taxes for them elsewhere.

Councils have special power to borrow from banks funds for local improvements. The loan must be repaid within the probable life of the work as certified by the engineer.

Where special assessments are irregular, new assessments may be made. But no assessment can be made or improvement undertaken unless it is initiated in some one of the three methods provided by law, namely:

(*a.*) Either on the report of the Engineer or other sanitary officer and of a committee of the Council recommending the proposed work or improvement for sanitary or drainage purposes adopted by the Council; or

(*b.*) On a petition of the owners of the real property benefited, sufficiently signed; or

(*c*) After due notice as above provided of the proposed assessment, and no petition of the owners of the real property benefited against the proposed assessment, sufficiently signed, being presented to the Council within the time limited therefor.

Property charged with local improvements is exempt from the general rates for the same purroses.

By-laws of a city, town or village in regard to drainage or local improvements need no advertisement or publication beyond written or printed notice being given to the owners, lessees or occupants or their agents. The notice must contain (*a*) a general description of the property, (*b*) the nature of the proposed improvements, (*e*) the estimated cost, (*d*) the amount of the assessment on the particular piece of property, (*c*) the time and mannor in which the same is payale, and (*f*) the time of the sitting of the Court of Revision. It must be signed by the Cerk or Aassessment Commissioner (see page 80) or other officer appointed by the

Council for the purpose. It must be mailed to the owner's address at least 15 days before the day appointed for the sittings of the Court of Revision; ten days' notice of the sittings must also be given by publication in some newspaper having a general circulation. This latter notice must specify generally what such assessment is to be for, and the total amount to be asssessed.

The above directions are sufficient for enabling any one to draw these notices. There can not be a general form given.

As stated above, property charged with local improvements is exempt from general rates for the same purposes but the cost of works at the intersection of streets is not included in this exemption; nor is such property exempt from such portion of the general rate as may be imposed to meet the cost of like works opposite real property which is exempt from such special assessment.

The following provisions of the statute are also made with reference to these exemptions:

"Where a local improvement or service is petitioned for and the petition is by two-thirds in number of the owners of the real property fronting or abutting upon the streets or place wherein or whereon such improvement or work is proposed to be done or made, the exemption may be for a specified period named in the petition and agreed to by the Council.

"Or if, with or without naming any period for such exemption the petition requests an arbitration the Council may accede to the proposal for an arbitration.

"In case the matter is to be determined by arbitration, a sole arbitrator shall be chosen for the purpose by the County Court Judge unless some person or persons is or are agreed to in that behalf by the petitioners and the Council.

"Wherever, by reason of a special assessment, the owners are exempted from a general rate for the like purpose, as aforesaid, the Council shall, from year to year, by by-law directing the general rate of assessment, or by some other by-law, state what proportion of the general rate is for purposes for which there is such special assessment in any part of the Municipality, and shall state the same in such manner as may give effect to this section.

"Until a by-law is passed containing such statement, none of the money raised by general rate on real property specially assessed or rated for any work or service hereafter executed shall be applied to any work or service of the same character in any part of the municipality."

A very important enactment was made by the Legislature in the year 1880, by virtue of which a city, town or village Council may, with the assent of the electors, pass a general by-law that all future expenditure for drainage and for purposes such as are mentioned on page 179 shall be by special assessment on the property benefited.

Such a by-law, after it is passed, cannot be repealed without the like assent of the electors; and in the case of such repeal, property which has become subject to a special rate by virtue of the by-law shall remain exempt from general rates. The time the exemption is to cease is to be determined by arbitration, and the arbitrator is to be appointed by the County Judge on application of the Council.

Where a general by-law has been passed as to local improvements such as mentioned in the second preceding paragraph, places of worship may be assessed like other property. These places may also be assessed where there is no such general by-law, but where under the ordinary plan of local improvement, two thirds of the owners of the real property (excluding the trustees, corporation or other persons in whom the church property is vested) and representing at least one half in value of the remaining property, petition the Council to undertake the said improvement.

Or, the trustees or others in whom the church property is vested may petition, along with others, for the local improvements. In such a case it is sufficient if the two thirds in number and one half in value, include the trustees and the church property respectively.

The intersections of streets, etc., may be charged on general rates in cases where special assessments are made for local improvements.

Local improvement debentures do not require the assent of the electors, otherwise than as declared in this chapter; the petition of the requisite proportion of ratepayers is necessary as described in the various cases, but no voting on any by-law is required. Nor is voting required where debentures are issued for the cost of improvement of intersection of streets, etc., as above mentioned.

Neither do local improvement debentures, where the assessment is special, form part of the general debt of the municipality within the meaning of restrictions which are in the case of some cities, etc., aid upon them, limiting the amount of debt which they can create. Nor is it necessary to recite debts for local improvements, in certain money by-laws in which it is ordinarily required to recite each and every amount of indebtedness of the municipality, but when these debts are not recited it must be stated that the amount of the general debt is exclusive of local improvement debts. See page 97.

As to sweeping, lighting and watering streets, it is provided that Councils of cities, towns and villages may pass by-laws for raising, upon the petition of at least two-thirds of the freeholders and householders resident in any street, square, alley or lane, representing in value one-half of the assessed real property therein, such sums as may be necessary for sweeping, watering or lighting the street, square, alley or lane, by means of a special rate on the real property therein according to the frontage thereof; but the Council may charge the general corporate funds with the expenditure incurred in such sweeping, watering or lighting.

The Council may also by by-law, define certain areas or sections within the municipalities in which the streets should be watered, swept and lighted and may impose a special rate upon the assessed real property, according to the frontage, in order to pay any expenses incurred in watering, sweeping or lighting such streets.

DIVISION III.—COUNTY BY-LAWS FOR ROAD IMPROVEMENTS.

County Councils have (in addition to powers mentioned in chapter XI) power to pass by-laws for levying on particular properties benefited a sufficient sum for making, repairing or improving any road, bridge or other public work in a township or between parts of two townships.

Firstly, the requisites of such a by-law are that a petition must be signed by at least two-thirds of the electors who are rated for at least one half of the value of the property within those parts of the township affected by the by-law, and secondly,—a printed notice of the petition, with the names of the signers, must be posted up and published for at least one month by putting up the same in four different places within such parts of the township, and also at the places for the sittings of the Council of each township. It must also be inserted weekly for three consecutive weeks in some newspaper in the county town. If there is no such newspaper then in the two newspapers published nearest the proposed work.

A County Council has also power to pass by-laws acquiring roads, etc., lying within one or more townships, towns or villages, and to levy special rates for the improvement of such roads, etc.

Such by-laws must state the amount to be raised for such work, and define the municipalities affected, and the portion of work to be performed by each municipality; provision is to be made for raising of the amount by county debentures payable in 20 years, or by equal annual instalments of principal with interest. An annual special rate is to be levied on all rateable property lying within the section defined in the by-law, which rate is to be sufficient for the payment of principal and interest of the debentures.

A by-law of this kind must receive the assent of the electors. In such municipalities as it carries it will apply to ; where it is not carried by the electors, the municipality will not be affected. The amount of money mentioned to be raised in the by-law is to be reduced by the proportionate amount which the municipalities voting against the by-law would have been required to pay.

Though as stated in the preceding paragraph, the by-law applies to such municipalities where it is carried, still where it is carried in some and lost in other municipalities, it is furthur requisite that the majority of the representatives of the municipalities carrying it, must vote for it in the County Council. These representatives only have the sole power in reference to the expenditure of the money to be raised by the by-law.

As to passing such by-laws generally, and voting on them by electors see Chapter VI.

The great difficulty with regard to local improvement is that ratepayers in such parts of a municipality as are not improved have objections to local improvements being carried out in parts where the improvements have been done at the general expense of the municipality for years. This has rendered the local improvement system rather unworkable.

CHAPTER XIII.

POWERS OF MUNICIPAL COUNCILS AS TO RAILWAYS.

All municipal Councils have a discretionary power to aid railways. The aid may be in any of the following ways:

1. By subscription for any number of shares in the capital stock of the company.
2. By lending money to the Company.
3. By guaranteeing the payment of any sum of money borrowed by the Company.
4. By endorsing or guaranteeing the Company's debentures.
5. Granting bonuses.

Debentures of the municipality for raising money for above purposes must be for not less than $20, and with or without interest.

The assent of the electors is necessary. See chapter VI.

There may be conditions attached to aid given by a municipality to a railway company.

By-laws of this kind come under the head of "By-Laws creating debts," as to which see page 96.

Where a City corporation passed a resolution granting $1,000 to an individual in consideration of his having advanced that amount in aid of a railway, the resolution was quashed.

In case a municipal corporation subscribes for and holds stock to the amount of $20,000, the head of the Council is *ex officio* one of the Directors of the Company, and has the same powers and duties as other Directors.

Township Councils may authorize any Railway Company to make a branch railway on corporation property or on highways, under such conditions as the Council sees fit. Power may also be granted by them to authorize companies or individuals to construct tramways and other railways *along* any highway on such terms and conditions as the Council sees fit.

The grouping of municipalities to aid railways, is a system which was abolished by the Municipal Act of 1883.

INDEX.

ADMINISTRATION OF OATHS—
    power to administer, 82.
    must relate to office, 82.
    as to accounts, etc., 82.
    distinction between oaths, affirmations and declarations, 83.

ALLEYS—
    See Streets.

ALMSHOUSES, 121.

ANIMALS—
    cruelty to, 127.
    fouling of docks, wharves, etc., by, 120.

ANTICIPATORY APPROPRIATIONS, 103, 104, 105.

APPRENTICES—
    preventing the sale of drink to, 130.

ARBITRATIONS —
    appointment of arbitrators to be by by-law and under sale, 106.
    time within which to be made, 106, 107.
    who to appoint, 106.
    between municipalities, 106.
    between corporations and individuals, 106.
    mode of procedure, 106.
    failure to appoint, 107.
    time for making award. 107.
    persons disqualified as arbitrators, 107.
    oath of arbitrator, 108.
    time of arbitrators' meetings, 108.
    discretion as to costs, 108.
    notes of evidence to be taken by, 108.
    exception to this rule, 109.

AREA OF TOWNS AND VILLAGES—18, 21.
    of town, how reduced, 21.
    of villages, how increased, 18.
      "   "   " reduced, 19.

ASSESSMENT COMMISSIONERS—
    appointed in cities, 80.
    notice to be given to, instead of to clerk, 80.

ASSESSORS—

    Same persons may be appointed assessors and collectors, 80.
    need not be appointed annually, 80.

AUCTIONEERS—

    by-laws to license, 136.
    sales on public streets, 136.

AUDITORS—

    appointed annually, 81.
    must have no contract with corporations, 81.
    duties of, 81.
    audit in cities and towns, 82.
        " " other municipalities, 82.
        " " city of Toronto, 82.

AWARD—

        See Arbitration.

BALLOTS—

        See Elections.

BILLIARD AND BAGATELLE TABLES—

    licensing and regulating, 126.

BIRDS—

    by-laws to prevent destruction of, 127.

BLASPHEMOUS LANGUAGE—

    by-laws to prevent—130.

BONUSES—

    to manufacturers, 121.
    to railways, 188.

BOOMS—

    by-laws for protecting, 150.

BOUNDARIES—

    contraction or increase of municipalities, 18, 19, 21.
    establishing boundaries, 131.
    survey, how made, 131, 132.
        " must follow statute or be considered unauthorized, 131, 132.
    between municipalities in reference to highways and bridges, 159, 160.

BOWLING ALLEYS.

    by-laws for preventing or regulating, 130.

BRANCH RAILWAYS—189.

BREAD—
>by-law for seizing, when of light weight, 124.
>" that loaf should be stamped, 124.
>" to prevent the use of deleterious materials in making of, 147.

BRIDGES—
>of county may be assumed by villages, 156
>such bridges to be toll free, 156
>to be kept in repair, 156
>approaches to, for 100 feet, must also be kept in repair, 156.
>where County Council has exclusive jurisdiction over, 156, 157
>forming boundary lines between municipalities, 158.
>over river or stream over 100 feet wide, etc, 158.
>what is meant by a "river," 158.
>bridge may be a public nuisance, 158.
>between two counties or county and city, 158.
>Provincial, Ordnance or Dominion bridge, 160.
>obstruction on bridges, 163.
>aid may be granted to adjoining municipality to maintain bridges, 164.
>aid may be granted by local municipalities to counties to maintain, 165.
>counties may maintain bridges across rivers 100 feet wide, etc., 167.
>powers of townships as to, 168.
>bridge companies may be aided, 121.
>driving on, 122.
>
>>See *Highways*.

BRUSHWOOD—
>by-laws as to, 129.

BUILDINGS, by-laws regulating, 122, 140, 148.

BY-LAWS—
>The general method by which corporation act, 17, 85.
>granting of monopolies prohibited, 86.
>may be repealed, 86.
>exceptions, 86.
>how authenticated, 87.
>when they require the assent of the Lieut.-Governor, 87.
>objection by ratepayers, 87.
>voting on by electors, 88 to 95.
>notices to be published, 88, 89.
>different other requisites, 90, 90.
>qualification of voters, 91.
>oaths of voters, 91, 92, 93.

unmarried women and widows, 94.
necessary votes to carry certain by-laws, 94, 95
confirmation of by-laws, 95.
purchase of public works, 99.
registration of, 99.
by-laws creating debts, 100.
   restrictions as to these, 96, 97.
   debt must not extend beyond 20 years, 97.
   rule as to interest, 97.
   annual rate to be provided, 97.
   exception in regard to local assessment, 97.
   how principal and interest payable, 97, 98.
   notice requisite, 98.
   time for applications to quash, to be made, 100
   not necessary to recite local improvement debts, 184
by-laws respecting yearly rates,
   limit of rates, 100, 101
   rate to be on actual value, 101
   local municipality has no power to impose a rate in aid of a county rate, 101
   cases where there is a deficiency or excess, 102
   special provision as to debentures before 1st Jan. 1867, 102
      see particular subjects

CAB STANDS—143
      See Livery Stables.

CANDIDATE—
      See Elections.

CELLARS—142.
CEMETERIES—126, 127, 139
CENSUS, of villages, towns and cities, 18, 20, 122
CHARITIES, aiding of, 121
CIRCUSES, 129
CITIES, how a town becomes a city, 20
   number of Wards requisite, 21
   how increased, 21
      As to Powers, see particular headings.
CLERKS, duties of, as to elections,
      see elections.
   to issue warrant in case of vacancy in Council, 72
   duties of generally, 75
   absence or illness of, 73, 75
   to show books, records, etc, and furnish copies, 75
   returns to be made by, 76, 77, 78
   effect of returns not being made. 76, 78
   of cities and towns to be clerk of police courts, 110
COLLECTOR, and assessor may be same person, 80
   to return list of tax defaulters on 15th December, 80
   need not be appointed annually, 80
COMPENSATION TO MEMBERS OF COUNCILS, 66,
   for lands taken, 134, 163
CONTRACT, with corporation disqualifies a Councillor, 35
   with company of which Councillor is shareholder, 36

Councils, how composed in different municipalities, 30, 31, 32
    distinction between, and corporation, 30.
    meetings of, when held, 63, 66.
    notice of, 63.
    no business to be done, till declaration taken, 63.
    form of declaration, 31, 63, 64.
    election of Warden of County, 65.
    remuneration of members for attending meetings, 65
    conduct of business at meetings, 66
    rules as to quorum, 66
    summoning meetings, 66, 67
    refusal of presiding officer to put motion, 67
    presiding officer in absence of head of Council, 67
    rules of order, 68, 69, 70, 71
    vacancies in Councils, 71, 72
    resignation of members, 72
    case of full number of members not elected, 73
    duties of heads of Councils, 74
Counties, how formed, 25
    senior county, where court house and gaol, 25
    how union may be dissolved, 25
    old by-laws to remain in force, 27
    exceptions to this rule, 27
    improvements by either county of a union, 151
        As to powers, see particular headings
Court Houses, Gaols, etc, duty of keeping in repair, 112
    inspection of gaols, 112
    duties of counties, cities, etc, as to court houses, 115, 116
    agreement as to, 116
    furniture, 116
Creditors, not affected by change in municipality, 27
Criminals, apprehension of, 124
Cruelty to Animals, 127
Debentures, guarantee of by county, 150
Declarations, distinction between and affirmations, 83
        See Forms.
Defaulters, in taxes, 125
Deputy Reeves, form of declaration, 31
    number of, 32
    number of, how increased, 27
Deputy Returning Officers,
        see elections.
Disqualification of members of Councils, 34, 35
    list of persons disqualified, 34, 35
    contracts with corporation, 35
    agent of contractor not disqualified, 36
    but partner is, 35, 36
    shareholders in companies, rules as to 36
    time from which disqualification dates, 36
    after election, 71, 72
Dogs, by-laws as to, 127
Drainage—requisites as to by-laws relating to, 98
    powers to open, make, preserve, etc, 122

and sewerage in cities, towns, etc, 142
tile, stone and timber drainage, 149
by-laws for deepening, straightening, etc, 171
requisites of, 171
embanking, pumping, etc, 171
appeals to court of revision, 173
work extended to adjoining municipality, 176
obstructions to, 176
town line ditches, 177

DRIVING—on roads and bridges, 122
on sidewalks, 139

ELECTIONS, nominations, 38
" time and place of holding, 38
" who to preside at, 38
" returning officer not present, 39
" candidates must be proposed and seconded, 40
" may resign when, 40
" if nominated for two offices, 40
time and place of election, 40
term of office, 40
first elections in new municipalities, 40, 41
by-law the proper method for appointing place of, 41
place of first election in junior township appointed by the County Council, 41
every election must be within municipality, 42
not to be in tavern, etc., 42
voters, 42
who are qualified, 43
resident, definition of, 44
farmers' sons, rules relating to, 44
tax defaulters, 44, 45
voters' list final, 45
misdescription of voters, 45
in case of addition of new territory, 45, 46
owners and occupants severally rated, 46
joint owners, etc., 46
returning officers and deputy-returning officers, 46
the clerk acts for the whole municipality, 46
appointment by by-law, 46
death of or failure to attend, 46
where none appointed, 46
are conservators of the peace, etc., 47
must not be partizan, 47
oaths, forms of, 47, 48, 49, 50, 51
who may issist on oath being administered, 51
no enquiries to be made, beyond oath, 51
refusal of officer to administer, 51,
the polling, 52
ballot-boxes and papers to be procured, 52
separate sets of papers when required, 52, 53
separate compartment for voters, 53,
printed directions for voters to be posted up, 53

voters' lists, 53
in case of first elections and of new territory, 53, 54
deputy-returning officers, poll clerks and agents may vote where stationed, 55
ballot-box to be opened, then locked and sealed, 55
duties as to entry of voters' names, etc., 55, 56
spoiled ballot papers, 56
who to be present in polling booths, 56
close of the poll, 56, 57
counting of ballots, 57
objections to ballots, 57,
statement and certificate of deputy-returning officer, 57, 58
agents of candidates may seal packets, 59
return of voters' list, 59, 60
dispute as to result, 60
declaration of result by clerk, how and when to be made, 60, 61
clerk to have the casting vote, 61
riot or other emergency, 61
clerk does not decide qualification of candidate, 61
ballot papers to be retained for one month, 61
destruction of ballot papers, 61
declaration of destruction to be made and filed, 62
inspection of ballot papers, 62
payment of expenses of election, 62
polling sub-divisions, making or changing, 125

EXEMPTIONS, persons exempt from serving in Council, 37
FAIRS—137
FARMERS' SONS—
    see elections.
FENCES, by-laws as to lawful fences, 128
 division fences, 128
 barbed wire fences, 128
 may be ordered to remove in winter, 128
FERRIES—130
FINANCES, accounts, how kept, 105
 investigation as to, 105
FINES AND PENALTIES—power to enforce, 128
FIRES—provisions in by-laws as to, 139, 140, 141
FORMS—of declaration of Reeve, 31
   "   Deputy-Reeve, 31
 oath of freeholder at elections, 48
  " income voter " 59
  " farmer's son " 51
  " deputy returning officer with voters' list, 59
 declaration of destruction of ballot papers, 62
    " office, 63, 64
    " qualification, 64
 affidavit of clerk attached to returns, 76
 oath of arbitrator, 108
 of notice, where voting on by-laws by electors, 89
 of authority of agent in voting on by-laws, 90

oath of freeholder voting on by-laws, 91
" leaseholder " " 92
" " " " relating to local improvements, 93
notice of confirmation of by-laws, 95
" by-law creating debts, 98
" publication of registered by-law, 100
" drainage by-law, 174
declaration of serving such notice, 175
oath of voting on drainage by-law, 178

FREE LIBRARIES—143
GAOLS—
see court houses
GUNPOWDER—139
HARBORS—obstructions to, 120
HAWKERS—136
HEAD OF THE COUNCIL—duties of, 74
HEALTH OF PUBLIC—133, 139
HIGH BAILIFF—in a city, 112
HIGHWAYS—what are deemed public, 154
    duty to repair, 155, 156
    road companies, 155
    widening of road, 156
    councillor knowing defect, 157
    where jurisdiction in counties, 157, 158
    boundary lines, 158, 160
    Provincial, Ordnance or Dominion road, 160
    ingress and egress to lands, 160
    width of roads and streets, 161
    stopping up, altering, etc, 161, 162
    to what extent tolls to be, 163
    timber on road allowances, 163, 165
    closing and selling road allowances, 163, 164, 169, 170
    substitution for original allowance, 164
    aid by one municipality to another, 164, 165, 169
    joint arrangement, 165
    township boundary lines, 165
    powers of county councils, 165 to 168
    double tracks in snow roads, 168
    mineral rights on or under roads, 169
    trees obstructing, 167, 169
HORSE RACING—130
    thieves, 135, 136
HOUSES OF CORRECTION AND INDUSTRY—
see court houses, etc.
HOUSES, of ill-fame, 130
HUCKSTERS—147
INDECENCY—by-laws to prevent, 130, 131
INDUSTRIAL FARMS—114
INSANE, destitute persons, 151
INTELLIGENCE OFFICES—147
INVESTIGATION—into finances, 105
    into conduct of officials, 117

JUNK STORES—138
LIQUOR LICENSES—sale of liquor to child, etc, 130
    limiting tavern and shop licenses, 184, 185
    numbering tavern and shop licenses, 184
    requiring better accommodation, 184
    apportionment of license fees, 185
    power to increase " " 185
    license fees must be uniform, 185
LIVERY STABLES—powers of Police Commissioners as to 112
         " towns and villages as to, 150
         " counties as to, 150
LOCAL IMPROVEMENTS—requisite in by-laws for local assessments, 97
    to what cases special assessments apply, 179
    proportion of petitioners, 179
    procedure, 179, 180, 181
    insufficient assessment, 180
    parties interested furnishing funds, 180
    common sewers, 180
    corner lots, 180
    lands unfit for building purposes, 180
    bridges and culverts, 180
    parties improving their own sidewalks, 180
    property rated for local improvements exempt from general rates, 181, 182
    general by-law for local improvements, 183
    places of worship, 184
    intersections of streets, 184
    assent of electors not required, 184
    not necessary to recite in money by-laws, 184
    county by-laws for road improvements, 185, 186
LOCK-UP HOUSES—113
MANUFACTORIES—aiding of, 121
MARKETS—144, 145, 146
MEAT—inspection of, etc, 143, 147
MILEAGE—of members of Councils, 66
MILK—inspection of, 143
NOMINATIONS,
        see elections.
NUISANCES, 139
NUMBERING HOUSES, 141
OATHS,
    see forms and administration of oaths.
PEDDLARS, 136
POLICE OFFICE, MAGISTRATE, COMMISSIONERS, ETC., each city and town must have police office, 110
    duty of Police Magistrate, 110
    when Justice of the Peace or Mayor to act, 110
    clerk of cities and towns to be Clerk of Police Court, 110
    salary of Police Magistrate, 110
    how appointed, 110, 111
    board of Police Commissioners, 111

town may dissolve boards, 111
pawers of boards, 111
" " as to livery stables and cabs, 111
power of Mayor to suspend constables, 111, 112
POLLING,
    see elections.
POUNDS AND POUND KEEPERS, 133
PROPERTY, obtaining by corporations, 119
    injuries to, 129
PROVISIONAL CORPORATION, 25, 33
PUBLIC HEALTH, 132
PUBLIC WORKS, purchase of, 99
QUALIFICATIONS, what are requisite, 33, 34
    property may be in right of wife, 34
    owner need not have deed in his name, 34
    free from encumbrance, 34
    see also "errata"—page 16
    assessment roll the guide, 34
    leasehold must be tenancy for a year, 34
    clerk does not decide as to qualifications, 34
    see also disqualification
RAILWAYS, AID TO, limit of two cents in the dollar not to apply to by-laws, 101
    by-laws to aid, 188, 189
    method of doing so, 188
    head of Council to be a director, in certain cases, 188
    branch railways, 189
    grouping system abolished, 189
ROAD COMPANIES, aiding of, 121
ROADS,
    see highways and local improvements,
SALARIES OF OFFICERS, compensation to members of Councils, 66
    how salaries provided for, 83
    no office to be let out by tender, 83
    gratuity to officers of 20 years' standing, 84
SCHOOLS, erection of, etc., 126, 137
SEWERAGE,
    see drainage
SLAUGHTER HOUSES, 138, 139
STATUTE LABOR, 152, 170
SUMMARY REMEDY for infraction of by-laws, 125
SURETIES OF OFFICERS, 29
STREETS, and squares, in considering area of village, 18, 19
    obstruction of, 141
    naming, 142
    width of, 161,
    sweeping, lighting and watering, 185. *see highways*
TAVERN—keeper of, disqualified, 35
    no election to take place in, 42
    see liquor licenses.
TELEGRAPH POLES—143
TEMPERANCE LAWS—124

Towns—how formed, 20
    area of, how reduced, 21
    wards of. how arranged, 22
    separation of, from county, 22
    results of separation, 22,
    old by-laws to remain in force, 27
    exceptions to this rule, 27
    re-union with county, 23
    how Council in is composed, 32
        as to powers see particular headings.
Townships—how formed, 23
    when junior township can separate, 24
    number of residents required, 24
    how junior township may be detatched from union
        and annexed to another municipality, 24
    old by-laws to remain in force, 27
    exceptions to this rule, 27
    how divided into wards, 41, 42
        as to powers see particular headings.
Transient Traders, 126
Treasurer—security by, 79
    sureties in case of change of corporation, 29
    duties of, generally, 179
    not to pay money to member of Council, 79
    must make half-yearly statement of assets, 80
Trees—ornamental, 123, 129
    obstructing highways, 167, 169
Vacant Lots—139
Vagrants—131
Victualling Houses—126
Villages—how formed, 18
    census may be taken, 18
    name, how given, 18
    area of, how increased and lessened, 18, 19
    what by-laws in force in added territory, 27
    when lying in two counties, 18
    how debts settled between them and county, 19. 28
    how it may cease to be incorporated, 19, 20
    annexation of, to other municipalities, 19, 20
    partly in two townships. 170
        as to powers see particular headings.
Voters—*see elections—see also by-laws*
Warden—election of, 65
    resignation of, 72
Wards, how arranged in towns, 32
    new division of, elections in such case, 41
    cease to exist in townships after separation 41
    how a township is divided into wards, 42
Water, supply of, 124, 130, 138, 149
Weeds, by-laws to prevent. 128
Wharves—powers as to, 120
Workhouses, 121

www.ingramcontent.com/pod-product-compliance
Lightning Source LLC
Chambersburg PA
CBHW020934230426
43666CB00008B/1675